WORK, PRODUCTIVITY, AND HUMAN PERFORMANCE

WORK, PRODUCTIVITY, AND HUMAN PERFORMANCE

Practical Case Studies in Ergonomics, Human Factors and Human Engineering

By

T. M. FRASER, M.D., M.Sc., PE, FACPM

Former Professor and Chairman
Department of Systems Design Engineering
and Director
Centre For Occupational Health and Safety
University of Waterloo, Ontario, Canada

and

P. J. PITYN, B.Sc., MEng., Ph.D.

Consultant
Former Associate Director
Centre For Occupational Health and Safety
University of Waterloo, Ontario, Canada

CHARLES C THOMAS • PUBLISHER
Springfield • Illinois • U.S.A.

Published and Distributed Throughout the World by

CHARLES C THOMAS • PUBLISHER
2600 South First Street
Springfield, Illinois 62794-9265

© *1994 by* CHARLES C THOMAS • PUBLISHER

ISBN 0-398-05910-1

Library of Congress Catalog Card Number: 94-6168

Printed in the United States of America
SC-R-3

Library of Congress Cataloging-in-Publication Data

Fraser, T. M. (Thomas Morris), 1922–
    Work, productivity, and human performance : practical case studies
in ergonomics, human factors, and human engineering / by T. M. Fraser
and P. J. Pityn.
        p.   cm.
    Includes bibliographical references and index.
    ISBN 0-398-05910-1
    1. Human engineering—Case studies.   2. Performance—Case studies.
I. Pityn, P. J.   II. Title.
TA166.F74   1994
620.8—dc20   94-6168
                                                                                      CIP

PREFACE

Work today is very different from what it was a century ago. It is no less demanding, no less fatiguing, no less stressful. In fact, although the nature of the stress may be different, the actual stress level may be even greater. Productivity is higher, but not necessarily because people work harder. The major difference in productivity derives from the concepts and practices of specialization of labor, the availability of relatively cheap supplemental energy, the standardization and interchangeability of parts and components, and the development of mass production and consumer demand. As a corollary, although not always a prime consideration, workers work shorter hours, usually in better working conditions, and generally with higher productivity. Optimum productivity, however, depends on developing the optimum relationship between the demands of the work and the capacity of the worker. Commonly, the demands of the work are predetermined while the capacity of the worker can be changed but little. Consequently, often the only way to improve the productivity, and at the same time improve the lot of the worker, is to so modify the interface between task and operator that even although the inherent capacity of the worker may be unchanged the productivity is nevertheless enhanced. As is explained in the Introduction to this book, it is the function of ergonomics to study human performance at work by evaluating work demands, analyzing human capacities, and attempting to match the one with the other.

In this book, through the study of carefully selected case histories, each based on a real-life problem, we attempt to show how a manager, whether in production, human resources, health and safety, or whatever, can use ordinary common sense, a little knowledge, and some people skills, to solve what otherwise might be nagging problems in human performance at work.

And while we happen to be specialists in areas including occupational medicine, engineering, ergonomics and occupational hygiene, we want to make it clear that for ordinary purposes a manager doesn't need all these skills to deal with problems in human performance. There may be times when a professional in these areas is required, but for screening, and ordinary day-to-day human problems, all you need to do is look, speak, listen, and then act. Look at your problems with different eyes; speak to anyone who has anything relevant to say, whether line management, staff, or on the shop floor; listen and evaluate what they are saying in the light of your observations and knowledge, and then act accordingly.

We hope that these case studies may guide you in what you can do.

T.M.F.
P.J.P.

ACKNOWLEDGMENTS

The authors wish to thank Mike Pityn of Pragma Mechanical Designs Ltd., Calgary, Canada for his skilled work in preparing the line illustrations and many of the figures in this text and to Martin King of University Hospital, London, Canada for computer resources and skills he provided. Their contributions are greatly appreciated.

CONTENTS

WORK, PRODUCTIVITY, AND HUMAN PERFORMANCE

INTRODUCTION TO CASES

To a physicist, work is a clearly defined entity represented by the product of the force applied to a body times the distance through which that body is thereby moved. That's all very well for a physicist, but for the rest of us it is very clear that the way we earn our living is work, whether it involves applying force to nearly immovable objects, or struggling to solve a nearly impossible problem. For the rest of us, in fact, the meaning of work is easily understood although it is not so clearly defined. For an athlete, work may encompass the arduous training he or she must undergo to achieve a permanent place on a team; for a TV casting agent it may be taking the beautiful people out to dinner, while for an industrial manager it may involve battling with paper, persons, and policies in an unending struggle towards the ultimate goal of productivity. One of the obstructions to optimum productivity, however, lies in the limitations of human performance. The capacity of people to perform tasks depends on basic human abilities, enhanced by education, training, selection, and direction. Education and training allow us to convert these basic abilities to skills. Selection and direction ensure that these skills are applied to the most appropriate tasks. But if the tasks, the work places, the tools and the equipment are not suitable to the worker, the resulting mismatch will inevitably lead to poor quality work, excessive worker fatigue, and lowered productivity.

Fitting of the task to the worker is known variously as ergonomics, human factors and human engineering. It is the purpose of this book to examine the applications of these disciplines to various problems that might be encountered in a variety of industrial and other situations. First, however, it would be wise to define and describe the words in question.

ERGONOMICS

Ergonomics can be considered as the study of the interrelationships that exist among the worker, or operator, his or her tools and equipment, and the environment in which the work or operation takes place. The word itself derives from two Greek words, *ergos,* meaning work, and *nomos,* meaning laws. In other words, the term *ergonomics* refers to the laws of work. It can be looked at as dealing with the anatomical, psychological, and physiological characteristics of a person that influence or determine the design and use of a workplace, a work station, and/or an operation, and with ensuring that the design of the associated task, tools, equipment, and procedures is compatible with the human limitations and capacities of the user.

Ergonomics, then, is not so much a discipline as an application. It is rooted in the disciplines of physical anthropology (anthropometry), human psychology, work physiology, and industrial or systems engineering, and because of this diversity it is transdisciplinary in its approach. Ergonomists, the practitioners of ergonomics, use the techniques and practices imported, developed and/or refined from the supporting disciplines to accomplish their ends. They use, for example, the concepts and techniques of anthropometry, which concerns the study of human dimensions, to determine the physical capacities and limitations of operators or other workers in terms of such measures as stature, reach, grasp and so on. These measures define the ideal dimensions of a work station in relation to age, gender and even ethnic background. They use the concepts and techniques of psychology to determine the human capacity to read and interpret information from dials, displays, and other sources, and to operate controls and equipment; and they use the results of these determinations to design the displays, controls, equipment, procedures, and workplace layout so that these are compatible with the human capacities so defined. They use the concepts and techniques of work physiology to evaluate the human capacity to undertake work, to lift and carry, to understand the significance of circadian rhythms and the need for rest, and to so design the work and work procedures that the work can be efficient and productive while still being conducted in health, safety and comfort.

HUMAN FACTORS, HUMAN ENGINEERING

There is often some confusion with respect to the meaning of the terms ergonomics and human factors engineering, or sometimes just human factors, or even human engineering. In fact, the differences, while real to their practitioners, are subtle, and perhaps not too significant from the practical point of view. Indeed, the term ergonomics is becoming widely accepted throughout the world as encompassing all that is meant by the three terms.

The term human factors originated in the U.S. during World War II, where its practitioners were originally concerned with ensuring that the design of aircraft and military vehicles was compatible with the capacities and limitations of the operators who were required to use them. Its concepts derived largely from those of psychology. Inevitably, however, the study of human factors, as well as its sources, developed into other areas and spread to other applications, until it became almost indistinguishable from ergonomics. The differences, indeed, although they stimulate much discussion among their proponents, are really academic now.

But still another term requires consideration before we move on, although it does not come within the context of ergonomics or human engineering. That term is occupational, or industrial, hygiene. The American Industrial Hygiene Association, one of the authoritative world bodies in occupational hygiene, defines occupational hygiene as: "That science and art devoted to the recognition, evaluation, and control of those environmental factors and stresses, arising in or from the workplace, which may cause sickness, impaired health and well-being, or significant discomfort and inefficiency among workers or among the citizens of the community." Like ergonomics, it too is transdisciplinary in its approach. It takes its origins in chemistry, chemical engineering, physiology, toxicology, and industrial engineering, although it has spread beyond these bounds until now it may also encompass elements which are perhaps more properly covered by or more historically considered to fall within the purview of ergonomics.

However, regardless of what you want to call the area of study, each discipline is concerned with the same thing, namely, trying to better the lot of the worker in the workplace with the ultimate objectives of maintaining health, ensuring safety, improving productivity, and if possible increasing human comfort. So, under the general rubric of ergonomics, let us see how we can apply some of the its concepts to conditions in the real world.

THE CASE STUDIES

As noted above, ergonomics is a transdisciplinary science, and its applications of necessity are essentially practical. Thus, while one can learn the relevant theory from the parent disciplines, and the approaches to application of that theory from ergonomic or human factors texts, much of the practice of ergonomics can really best be learned only by exposure to actual situations in the field. While this is undoubtedly the best way, it is unfortunately not always feasible, but the examination of prepared case studies such as those within this text is perhaps one of the next best things.

The authors, therefore, invite you to a series of exercises in ergonomic problem solving, and hope that in considering them you are challenged intellectually, as well as stimulated to learning in a way that is enjoyable. We hope, also, that you will be provoked into thinking of ergonomic solutions to problems you might otherwise have ignored. Consequently, we present a group of case studies for your consideration and action. In each case study a situation is outlined in some detail—in sufficient detail in fact for you to understand the problem and its background, and to make meaningful recommendations as to a possible solution. At the end of each case study there is an assignment that you are asked to consider on the basis of the information provided for you. Some of these problems derive from the factory shop floor or warehouse, some from the office or marketplace, some from compensation insurance and human rights legislation, while some indeed are more concerned with evaluation of the ergonomic aspects of job demand than with design for human use. The scenarios may speak to a different time or a different place, yet there should be aspects in each that will be familiar to you in some way. Thus, we hope that not only will the problems and solutions hold your interest but that the narrative, commentary, and background will compensate, to some extent at least, for the lack of the hands-on experience that you might gain in the field. All the facts relevant to the study are presented in each case. In addition, the appendices provide some statistical and other supporting information of value in presenting the solution. For more comprehensive information you may need to research the subject matters further.

Keep in mind that we have sought to provide a variety of problems, each one different, and each illustrating one or more aspects of ergonomics or human factors engineering. The cases are written by specialist practitioners for readers who are interested in solving problems they face at work, for students at all levels, and for those with closely allied work and professional interests. The more knowledgeable the reader, the greater will be his/her capacity to deal with the problems presented. Ergonomics is in some ways universal, because solving human problems in the workplace is not of limited interest only to those with background in ergonomics but also to industrial managers facing high compensation levies, injured workers facing a troubling dysfunction and to a number of others concerned about productivity and performance. Often solutions can be found in the application of acquired common sense—a commodity which unfortunately is often in short supply. It is our hope, of course, that the material will be of value as a broad teaching and training instrument, in the classroom and in industry alike, to instructors and students alike, and to practitioners in various closely related disciplines. Teachers especially may be interested in extracting material from the problem sets, or creating their own using the scenarios developed.

In working through each case study the reader should always keep in mind the question, "What is the simplest solution?" Complex, sophisticated solutions can often be suggested for what may really be relatively simple problems, but these solutions may not necessarily be the most appropriate, nor the most feasible, for a variety of reasons, not the least of which is determined by the money available. Readers are asked, therefore, to place themselves in the position of the persons to whom the case pertains, and to recognize that these persons usually have very real constraints, whether or not these are specifically stated.

The authors do not profess to have all of the answers, nor even the right answer, nor can all the cases be described in the detail that some readers might like. With these limitations in mind, however, you are asked to participate as fully as you can, bringing your knowledge, imagination and creative talents to the study of what we hope are cases which are both informative and stimulating.

We want you to read each case study carefully. Read it once to get an overview of the situation. Then read it again to get the details. Determine clearly what is required of the assignment you will find at the end of each case study. Take note—of dates, dimensions, whatever seems significant. *But don't read the solution until you have prepared the assignment.*

You will gain much more by preparing the assignment first. After you have prepared your solution, read ours. And remember, we do not necessarily present the only answer, nor even the right answer. We merely present what our knowledge and experience has shown to be appropriate. And that doesn't mean that you can't do better.

We apologize for any errors and oversights which might muddle the picture. Indeed, we would be pleased to hear about these and will endeavor to correct them in the future should the occasion arise.

Finally, you should recognize that it is your own active involvement and input which will determine how useful and meaningful this material is going to be to you. Therefore, make the most of it!

Case I

THE HANDICAPPED MEAT PROCESSOR

INTRODUCTION

A problem facing many employers today is how to meet the social and legislative demands for employing the handicapped. It is not so long ago that an employee who received a disabling injury on or off the job was let go as soon as there was any doubt about his or her capacity to work. Similarly, a candidate for employment, with a greater or lesser degree of disability, was often rejected without further consideration.

Today, however, it is becoming incumbent on the employer to go out of his way to avoid discrimination against the handicapped and to ensure to the best of his ability, and even to his own disadvantage, that a handicapped worker can be provided with a meaningful job within his or her capacity.

This case is about a worker who was injured both on and off the job.

BACKGROUND

While some companies provide for injured workers by way of a private insurance scheme, the worker in this particular jurisdiction was covered under the provisions of a Workers' Compensation Act. Workers' compensation provides for automatic compensation for an injured worker except where there is willful misconduct, or the injury/illness is believed to be non-occupational in origin. The compensation is financed by a levy on all employers; the more claims awarded, the higher is the levy. Claims for compensation are submitted to a Workers' Compensation Board.

In addition, however, legislation in this particular jurisdiction now makes it mandatory for the employer to make provisions for employing the handicapped. The legislation guarantees equal treatment if the person is capable of performing or fulfilling the *essential duties* of the job. A person cannot be found incapable of performing those essential duties

9

unless an effort has been made to accommodate his or her needs. Each person must be considered individually.

THE COMPANY

Poultry Packers is a division of a large corporate food conglomerate. The division has several processing plants, each of which is more or less autonomous within the limitations of corporate policy. As with most companies, the prime objective is to be profitable while maintaining the corporate image and remaining within the spirit, or even the letter, of the law. In recent years, however, in the face of increasing competition and economic recession, company profits have been hard to come by.

The plant under consideration employs some 40 workers, male and female, most of whom are involved in the same type of task, namely, poultry processing. There are four maintenance workers and some clerical staff. All the hourly employees are members of the same trade union which is jealous of jobs and seniority as well as being active in health and safety matters. There are, however, no health services other than First Aid in the plant, and no divisional medical or nursing services.

Work is conducted on demand, with periodic layoffs as the demand slackens. The plant operates on a single-shift basis, with normal working hours from 7 A.M. to 4 P.M. and two 10-minute coffee breaks and one 1-hour lunch break.

THE WORK

The work comprises the slaughter, evisceration and trussing of whole turkeys. The sequence of tasks has been organized to provide the most efficient series of operations, beginning with a slaughtered bird hung on a hook and ending with a finished carcass trussed for packaging and retail. The slaughtered turkeys are brought into the work area suspended on hooks on an overhead conveyor line which winds through the room past various work stations. Below the line, at waist height, is a continuous bench on which the work stations are located. The bench includes a channel, or runnel, with flowing water which carries away waste. The bench is also used as a depository for tools and turkey parts. At each work station one or more of a number of many different types of specific operations are conducted as the turkeys go by. These operations include such esoteric procedures as neck slitting, crop pulling, viscera drawing and lung suctioning, to name a few. Depending on the particular task, the work may be relatively light, such as trimming or gizzard slitting, or it may be heavy and demanding such as crop pulling or trussing. Regardless of the work, however, the worker stands during the entire shift, commonly working with arms outstretched, or stretched upwards, processing the carcass or removing unwanted portions with much manipulation of the hands, arms and shoulders, along with, in many tasks, pulling and tugging at the suspended turkey. Considerable force may be required to complete many of the tasks. This force is in turn transferred to the back which undergoes repeated rotational and transverse flexional motions during the manipulation of the hands, arms, and shoulders, and to the legs which stabilize the back during its motions. It is often necessary also to shift weight from one foot to the other, sometimes when the foot is at an angle unsuitable for accepting the change in weight. At some stations the worker stands on a fixed raised platform, 6″–12″ high, in order to reduce the upward arm stretch. A worker may be assigned by the foreman to any station on the line. Because of the sequence of required operations there is no station where all the work is light. At any given station there may be a requirement for both light and heavy operations. There are, in fact, no defined light operations in the plant.

All the work takes place in one large room with concrete walls and floor. The work room is heated in cold weather, but may become excessively hot in summer. Large quantities of water are used during the processing for flushing carcasses, cleaning, transporting unwanted waste, and so on. The floor is continuously wet and puddled. In addition it is slippery with fat, blood, and other fluids, to the extent that care has to be taken to avoid slips and falls while moving.

THE WORKER

The worker with whom this case is concerned, Dave Marsden by name, is a 38-year-old Caucasian, married, with two children. His employment records show that he was hired by the company in 1980. At the time of hiring, according to his preemployment medical examination, he was fit, healthy, 70″ in height, and 165 lbs in weight. He had no significant history of illness or injury. Prior to hiring he had done municipal laboring jobs.

THE WORK HISTORY

Mr. Marsden's work record was unremarkable until February 11, 1987 when he was involved in a motor vehicle accident in which he suffered a severe crushing compound fracture of his right ankle. The injury required intensive surgical treatment, with hospitalization until May 18, 1987. At that time he was returned home, capable of walking but requiring continued medical treatment and physiotherapy. The injury was to a large extent healed but, because of impaired blood supply, the skin tended to ulcerate, and of course there was considerable reduction in mobility. With permission from the hospital and his doctors he returned to work on July 9, 1987.

He went back on the line and continued his work more or less uneventfully until January of the next year (1988). His employment records during that period reveal only a few absences for undefined medical appointments and casual sickness. On January 10, however, he submitted a medical certificate from the local physician to the effect that he needed to be off for some months for "rest and further treatment." As is often the case in such certificates, however, there was no further indication of the nature of his problem.

He returned to work again on April 8 of that year. During the subsequent eight months he is recorded as having several more medical appointments and sickness absences. On January 5, 1989, however, he submitted a further medical certificate indicating he would be off for another four or five months, and on February 8, 1989, he had an amputation of his right leg above the ankle.

Following a period of rehabilitation and treatment he was fitted with a prosthesis and returned to work in June 1989. His leg, however, continued to cause problems, although he remained at work with occasional short breaks.

On November 20, 1989, he had a fall while working. He stated that he was standing on one of the platforms, raised about 9 inches above floor level, when, as the turkeys advanced along the line, he inadvertently stepped off the end of the platform. First Aid records show that he reported the fall to the person in charge two days later, claiming that he had scraped the skin on his stump. He stated at that time that the accident was witnessed by two fellow employees, James Aker and Nancy Lewis. Medical records show that he reported the accident to his doctor one week after the incident. In a subsequent report, an investigator from the Workers' Compensation Board stated as follows: "We contacted Mr. James Aker and were advised that he did not witness any accident where you stepped off a platform and fell on your knees, although he learned about it later. Nancy Lewis told us that she did in fact see you inadvertently step off a high stand and fall to the floor and that you immediately went to First Aid for treatment."

After that accident his progress continued in much the same fashion as before, until March 22, 1990 when a medical certificate was received stating: "Mr. Marsden has stump swelling and complications related to the fit of his prosthesis, which requires further adjustment. It is recommended that he be removed from work for three weeks." He returned to work on April 16, 1990, but was again laid off with a medical certificate stating "[he is] not able to return for several months until a new prosthesis is fabricated." He returned on November 5, 1990 with a new prosthesis, but continued to have problems.

On March 5, 1991, a medical certificate was received from his personal physician stating as follows: "Mr. Marsden has been instructed to stop working due to the status of his stump." He has not worked since and has submitted a claim to the Workers' Compensation Board seeking full financial benefits.

The case was investigated by the Workers' Compensation Board who sent field investigators to interview Mr. Marsden and company representatives, including the persons already mentioned. They also obtained copies of all the relevant medical documentation, not normally available to the company. The medical documentation essentially confirmed in technical language the sequence of events already described as well as the opinions of the personal doctor, surgeon, and physical therapist on Mr. Marsden's fitness for work.

On August 14, 1991, Mr. Marsden received a letter from the claims adjudicator of the Workers' Compensation Board, stating in part:

"To consider the payment of compensation benefits for lost wages and health care expenses, it must be shown that the disability resulted from an accident arising out of and occurring in the course of employment. . . . It is not sufficient that the disability comes on during work. There must be something about the work which caused the disability to occur, such as strenuous work, an awkward position, an unaccustomed strain, or even a movement arising out of the work which could reasonably cause the disability. . . . "

After detailing the investigation the letter went on to say: "Based on the information we have on file, we are of the opinion that your present disability did not arise out of employment but was caused by your non-compensable amputation, therefore we are allowing entitlement for your initial treatment only, for damages suffered during your fall, but are denying entitlement for lost time and further health care benefits, as the disability is not related to the accident history given."

Human rights legislation in this jurisdiction requires that if Mr. Marsden is not fully compensated by the Workers' Compensation Board, the company must make provision for him to work even if he is handicapped.

ASSIGNMENT

Both the company and Mr. Marsden have the right to accept the decision or to submit an objection to it. Mr. Marsden has submitted an objection. As an ergonomist/health and safety specialist, you have been requested by the plant manager to prepare a report outlining what you think the company should do at this point. Your report should review the relevant circumstances and make recommendations, with appropriate justification, as to whether you think the company should accept the board's ruling or whether the company should also submit an objection requesting that Mr. Marsden receive much more in the way of compensation.

While these are some, although certainly not all, of the considerations, there are other facts and implications in the history that have to be considered, and indeed the real learning experience in this exercise is not so much concerned with finding a singular solution, as with learning how to organize and present the material in such a manner that a meaningful decision can be made.

THE HANDICAPPED MEAT PROCESSOR SOLUTION

There is of course no unique solution to this problem. Your view of the circumstances and your recommendations can be as valid as those of anyone else, so long as you can justify them. Consequently, no ideal report will be presented here. However, some of the considerations that you will have to bear in mind are discussed below.

If, for example, you decide to accept the decision, you will have to consider what Mr. Marsden is going to do now. He has been advised by his doctor to stop working. That, however, does not mean that he cannot do any work. Indeed, it might have been a ploy to assist him in gaining benefits. In any case, under human rights legislation you may be required to provide him with a job the essential duties of which are within his capacity. This in turn might mean offering him a less strenuous job than working on the line, or modifying a work station to meet his requirements. However, other than for the few maintenance workers, whose jobs are carefully guarded, there are no jobs outside of working on the line, although it might be possible to create one. But if you were to create one, it should be a meaningful job. There are few things more soul destroying for a worker than sitting in a corner pretending to work. Furthermore, would such a solution be acceptable as far as the law is concerned?

On the other hand, job modification does not offer much possibility either. For example, long usage has established that it is not practicable to do poultry processing from a seated position. Indeed, although working from a seated position might relieve some of Mr. Marsden's stump problems, it could and probably would create other potentially disabling shoulder and back problems from the extended reaches and awkward manipulations required in seated work. In addition, extensive changes would have to be made to the line to create a seated work station—a process which would certainly be expensive if indeed feasible. Consideration, however, might be given to a specially designed sit-stand station, raised to a suitable height from the floor, where Mr. Marsden could sit with his feet on the platform in such a manner that he could still do the essential duties of the task. Such a station would be not be unduly expensive and might well meet the requirements.

If, however, you believe that you cannot reasonably employ Mr. Marsden and consider that he would be better off on full permanent compensation, you might claim that the fall at work aggravated Mr. Marsden's existing problems to the extent of partial or full disability, although you might have some difficulty justifying that claim. If, as a result, Mr. Marsden received partial compensation, then, although your responsibility would now be less, you might still find yourself having to find him a job, perhaps part-time or under limited conditions. Of course, under these circumstances your required compensation levy would now increase, perhaps for years to come. If he were to receive total compensation, of course, the increase in levy would be even greater, although you would not be committed to finding him a job.

Case II

THE DAMAGED DRY GOODS

A large retail supplier in the food industry has found that too many dry goods leaving Number 3 plant are damaged. The source of the damage has not yet been identified. The problem at this time has been traced back only so far as the receiving area, which means that the goods could also be arriving damaged. However, the sentiment among management personnel and production coordinators is that the shipping/receiving department needs to be examined. The reasons for this may be speculative more than they are concrete, when one considers the current poor state of relations between the employees and the employer. There are those in management and production who have suggested that workers have a poor attitude and simply don't exercise enough care when handling the goods. As they see it, the job is simple. The job is to unload the pallets and load the conveyors, nothing more. What could be easier? Others have taken a less accusatory position, arguing that as performance slackens for whatever reason, the goods get handled more crudely. The latter are more hesitant to blame the workers directly, contending that workers tire and get bored towards the end of a shift of doing nothing but shuffling boxes.

There is, in fact, no doubt that relations between employees and management over the previous few years have had sundry ups and downs. Plant Number 3 employs a few of the more militant workers who have been vocal about management's handling of past affairs. Add to this that because of the current financial position of the company, which is well known to the employees, many of the shop floor workers are currently under considerable stress. Most are feeling threatened that the company's dismal financial performance this past year will have some negative impact, perhaps in loss of jobs, wage cuts, reduced hours or something of the sort.

PACKAGING PROCESS

Cookies (a term which includes here various sweet biscuits, cookies and crackers) arrive pre-wrapped in small individualized packets of four cookies to a packet. By combining different types of packets an assortment of snack packs is produced. Six different selections or assortments are packaged. The snack packs are convenient for lunches, little treats between meals, and for people on the move. The individualized wrapping assures freshness and easy portability.

The cookies are shipped separately in cardboard cartons according to type. There are ten different types. Some are sent from another plant for sorting and re-packaging, while others are made at Number 3 plant. They are all brought to the central receiving area where they are loaded on to a conveyor and whisked off to be repackaged. Central receiving coordinates the distribution and therefore acts as the front end of the packaging line.

Most of central receiving is a temporary holding zone, with only one active work area, the loading chutes. The layout of the workspace is fairly simple (Fig. II-1) and so is the work. Cartons filled with cookies are taken from wooden pallets and manually placed on to specific loading chutes, according to the type of snack pack being produced at the time. The loading chutes are nothing more than a continuous shelf partitioned off into five divisions, each leading to a separate conveyor belt. The cookies are fed on to their respective conveyor positions to be subsequently grouped and packaged into assortments.

EQUIPMENT AND MATERIALS

The cartons arrive stacked twenty-one to a pallet, arranged in three layers of seven. The cartons are all of the same size, measuring 17" in height, 15" in width, and 21" in length. Their weight varies according to the type of cookie contained therein (Table II–I). Light cream-filled wafers weigh as little as 14 lbs per carton, compared to 37 lbs per carton for the scrumptious cookies laden with chocolate chips, peanuts and raisins. Cartons have circular finger holes at the sides for grasping, the diameter of which is 2".

Cartons are standard cardboard boxes with flaps forming the top and bottom. The bottoms are stapled and taped for extra protection. The top flaps are folded cross-wise to secure the contents while allowing subse-

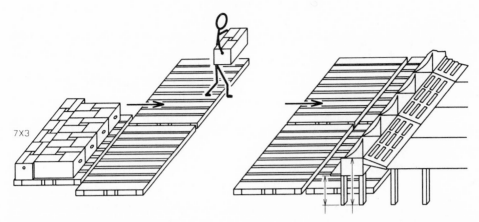

Figure II-1. A schematic of the work area showing the basic elements of this manual handling task. Cartons are lifted from the pallet and carried over to the loading chute, while treading over a makeshift platform made of empty wooden pallets. Pallets are stacked three cartons high when full. The pallet is shown two-thirds depleted.

Table II-I
CARTON WEIGHT IN RELATION TO COOKIE TYPE

Cookie	Weight (lbs)
A	22
B	14
C	17
D	29
E	29
F	17
G	37
H	28
I	21
J	17

Note: Average weight per carton: 22 lbs (10 kg)

quent access. The cartons are not otherwise sealed with tape or staples until after the re-packaging has been completed and the cookies are ready to be shipped out to buyers. Thus, the cartons essentially serve two similar functions, namely, as a temporary means of transporting goods to the packaging area and later as a shipping container.

To facilitate loading, each carton is placed on a shelf in front of the chutes. For repackaging and sorting, the cartons are opened before being loaded. Flaps are unfolded, the carton is turned on one end, lifted into place and set down, hopefully without dumping any cookies. The loading chute is at chest height, 47″ above the floor. The shelf on which the cartons are rested while they are being opened is at a height of 30″ between the floor and loading chute. The shelf protrudes into the path of the lift, 14½″ beyond the loading chute. It has an additional ½″ rubber lip covering the edge to prevent injury. The shelf makes it easier to open cartons, but makes subsequent loading more difficult.

To reduce the lifting distance, workers have laid down wooden pallets in front of the loading chutes to form a makeshift platform. The walking surface in front of the loading chutes is thus elevated by another 5″, the approximate height of the wooden pallets. There is an open floor area between the makeshift platform and the holding area.

MANUAL WORK

The sequence of loading cartons requires a nominal amount of planning and coordination, but otherwise the job involves only the manual transfer of cartons. Cartons are lifted from the pallet, usually by supporting the bottom edge of one side and holding on to the far corner on the other side, not by using the finger holes which are uncomfortable and exert too much localized pressure on small areas of the fingers. Cartons are carried from the pallet and placed on to the shelf in front of the loading chute. They are opened and rotated so that the narrow axis fits the loading chute. Then the cartons are transferred from the shelf to the loading chute using a combination of lifting and maneuvering. A certain amount of juggling is involved in lifting the cartons from the shelf, because the cartons are rotated on end while being loaded into the chute. The cartons are brought to rest on the edge of loading chute, then shoved into place. While the cartons stand rather precariously on their long axis (Fig. II-2), their contents are at risk of spilling out.

Workers are expected to handle sixty cartons of each type per shift, with the exception of type "G" (see Table II–I), of which they are required to handle only thirty. Workers spend one full week on the job before rotating to another position in the packaging department. Six different employees, male and female, participate in the rotation schedule.

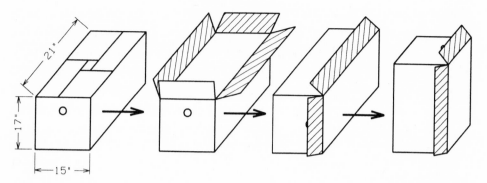

Figure II-2. Cartons are juggled during manual handling and rotated on to their sides leaving them in a precarious upright position.

ASSIGNMENT

The production manager believes that the attitude of the workers is the main cause of the problem, and considers that something should be done now, and that focussing on the quality of their work should be the priority. You've been asked by the company to investigate the handling of goods, with one caveat, namely, you must confine your investigation to the receiving department where the problems are believed to originate.

During preliminary discussions you've voiced your concern about such a narrowly defined study because of what you already know or intuitively sense about the political situation, but management is still only interested in a pared-down study. A more comprehensive study, you are told, is not warranted at the present time, although future possibilities of such are not altogether ruled out. The constraints are beyond your control. You've accepted them and moved on. Not knowing in advance what you might find, you've asked the production people for information on whether goods are being damaged in transit to Number 3 plant, whether more are damaged at the end of the shift than the beginning, and, since there is an assorted lot, whether one type is being damaged more than another, but management is not interested in these differences. They want to know only about work practices at the loading chute.

It will be clear that poor design of work station and procedures appear to be major factors contributing to fatigue and reduced performance. It is no insignificant feat to load the cookies without having them tumble out of the cartons as they reach the top of the chute and fall in damaged disarray on to the floor. Muscle fatigue from continued lifting with the arms in an outstretched position makes control even more difficult, while tripping during carrying is a potential hazard. How can the situation be improved? Investigate the work as far as you can from the information given and make recommendations on how to re-design the procedures and loading area to effect improvements.

Under the circumstances it would be judicious to evaluate the lifting requirements, making those findings known when presenting your recommendations. If the manual handling tasks indeed pose a problem, you will need to demonstrate this problem to management who seem to be convinced otherwise. Evaluate the task in a simplified manner assuming that there are two separate lifts, that is, lifting from pallet to shelf and from shelf to loading chute. Use the NIOSH lifting limits and other information provided in Appendices 2 and 3. Suppose the lifts could be modified, combining them into one. What effect would this have? What would it take to accomplish?

THE DAMAGED DRY GOODS SOLUTION

Before attempting a solution, or reading this solution, familiarize yourself with the NIOSH lifting guidelines outlined in Appendix 2 and those of Snook and Ciriello described in Appendix 3.

As a first estimate you might wish to determine the lifting demands of the average task, perhaps sparing you some additional unnecessary work. This would instinctively seem to be a reasonable approach. But, as the following explanation will show, problems may be encountered in oversimplifying the tasks. By assuming an average point of origin (V) for the lift to be at the middle of the intermediate layer, you can utilize the NIOSH guidelines to make a preliminary assessment of the demands incurred in lifting a carton from pallet to shelf. You may find your conclusions in error, if your calculations reveal the following:

Lift: Pallet to Shelf

The NIOSH formula in customary U.S. and metric units is as follows:

$\mathbf{AL}$ (lb) $= 90(6/H)(1-\{.01|V-30|\})(.7+\{3/D\})(1-F/F_{max})$

$\mathbf{AL}$ (kg) $= 40(15/H)(1 - \{.004|V-75|\})(.7 + \{7.5/D\})(1 - F/F_{max})$

For this lift:

$\mathbf{H}$ = 15″ carton width/2 + 6″ = 13.5″ (34 cm)
Assuming the carton is held to the body with a symmetrical two-handed lift, and adding 6″ for body thickness.

$\mathbf{V}_{avg}$ = 17″ carton height × 1.5 = 25.5″ (63 cm)
Assuming the average point of origin to be at the middle of the intermediate layer, *with the worker standing on the pallet while lifting,* i.e., pallet thickness not a factor.

$\mathbf{D}$ = destination − origin
   = 25 (30″ shelf height − 5″ platform) (62 cm) − V_{avg} at the origin
The platform effectively reduces D by 5″, resulting in a D_{avg} of

23

zero; literal meaning, cartons transferred from the middle layer are shuffled horizontally to the shelf without any lifting being performed.

F = (60 cartons × 9) + (30 cartons) per shift
= 570 lifts per 8 hr shift
= 1.2 to 1.5 lifts/min, depending on whether lunch and rest breaks are included.

Under these circumstances, assuming the average height of lift to be at the middle of the intermediate layer, then D is effectively zero, and no lift takes place. Consequently, the NIOSH Action Limit (AL) is zero. What does this mean? Literally, it means the average manual handling task so defined does not involve lifting. At first glance, this is odd but true. While D actually ranges from a value of +17″ to −17″ during unloading of the pallet, the shelf and the middle of the stack of cartons are both at the same height. Assessing the average condition, where D = 0, that is by oversimplifying the parameters, does not generate a useful analysis from the formula.

Using an approximation of the average limit for unloading the cartons can nevertheless be useful and can be done as explained below. The simplification describes a worker grasping the box midway along the sides, while unloading from the second tier of cartons. In practice, the finger holes are not used. Workers grab the cartons along the bottom edges and corners. The difference is a few inches but has no effect on the lifting limit. Legitimately, D should be set to a value other than zero, equal to even the smallest practical dimension, one inch. In fact, D cannot equal zero. One of the stipulations of the NIOSH formula is that D_{min} has a value of 10″ (25 cm) and anything less is assigned the minimum travel distance. Figure II-3 shows that when D < 10″ there is no devaluation of the limit. Furthermore, generally D exerts a relatively minor influence for most lifts.

In the example above, suppose that D was actually 8″, thus accounting for a more realistic grasp. There is no effect on the calculated Action Limit at D_{min}, although V, the point of origin, is slightly altered to account for the position of the hands at the start of lift. Accordingly, V would have a value of 17″ representing the average Point of Origin. The conclusion would remain the same, that the average manual handling demands of this part of task would appear to be acceptable.

The next step might be to consider how the various components differ when unloading from the top, middle or bottom tier. This situation is more complex than usual, because lifting is not the only activity being performed. Breaking down the unloading task into components gives the following three scenarios: one element constitutes a lift (transfer of cartons from the bottom layer), one involves a short lift but is primarily a horizontal transfer (transfer of cartons from the middle layer), and one actually constitutes a lowering maneuver rather than a lift. The question is how to handle three distinct activities, only one of which clearly constitutes a lifting maneuver falling within the NIOSH lifting parameters.

One approach might be to attempt the NIOSH calculation for all three components separately. In this case the actual values of V are 34, 17, 0 for unloading of cartons from the top, middle and bottom layers of the pallet. The corresponding values of D would be -14, 18, 26, respectively. One third of the F value shown above would be ascribed to each (0.5 lifts per minute) resulting in a very minor effect on the Action Limit. Even a cursory examination of the NIOSH factors is sufficient to illustrate that the lifts would comply with the NIOSH criteria for safe lifting.

As shown in Figure II-3 the size of the carton has the most significant effect on the lift. Even with depreciation of the limit by more than 50% due solely to the H factor, however, the task would still be acceptable for most workers. From an interventionist point of view, H (the carton) may not be easy to change, although it would be the most effective place to make changes.

It can also be ascertained from Figure II-3 that, in fact, none of the factors sufficiently reduces the limit to warrant further analysis, hence, the conclusion that the task is acceptable in and of itself. Nevertheless, this task must be viewed in relation to the second lifting task, a matter to be discussed shortly.

Taking another simple approach, an approximation of the physical demands of this task can also be obtained by comparing the required handling activities to those recommended in the Snook and Ciriello guidelines (Appendix 3). The guidelines cover lifting, lowering, and carrying. According to Snook and Ciriello, the lift is the critical activity. In this case, lifting cartons from the bottom layer represents the worst case lift. From Snook and Ciriello it can be determined, using F values corresponding to 1 lift/2 minutes, that the majority of workers are able to perform this part of the task satisfactorily. Likewise, you can assume that the worst case was evaluated while performing the NIOSH analysis, even though the task of *lowering* could not be specifically assessed.

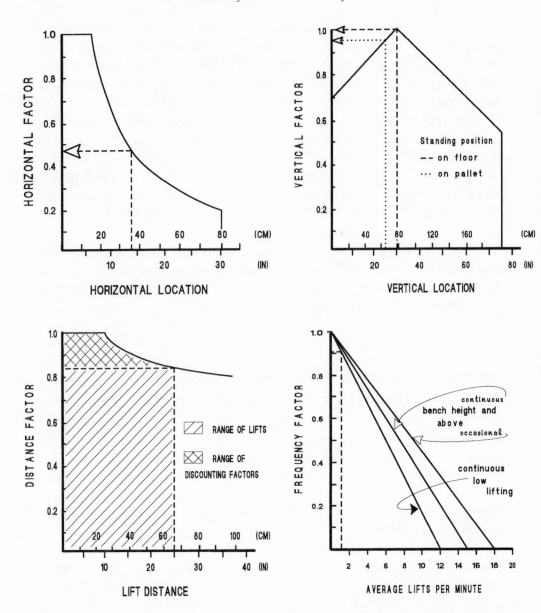

Figure II-3. The effect of the individual NIOSH lifting parameter on the Action Limit is shown in this multi-component illustration. Values for the horizontal and vertical points of origin, the travel distance and the lifting frequency are taken from the text and plotted along the horizontal axis. The influence of the respective lifting variables on reducing the limit is ascertained by reading the corresponding value from the Y axis. The horizontal factor has the smallest value of the group of four factors indicating that it alone accounts for a reduction in the limit of approximately one-half. Intervention would be most effective by tackling the horizontal displacement issue.

To get a composite estimate of the unloading task and/or to analyze the individual components, the Snook and Ciriello guidelines may be used as an alternative to the NIOSH method. This requires a certain amount of inference and interpolation between tabulated values. It has been established that the task in and of itself is acceptable and that the *average* condition is represented by cartons unloaded from the intermediate layer. Taking this as a point of reference, for comparing the different activities of lifting, carrying and lowering shows that the lifting represents the worst case, and carrying the average case. When assessing the physical requirements of the task, individually or collectively, use either the cumulative value for frequency, in this case 1 lift/minute, or a portion thereof, to determine the limits just as in the NIOSH analysis.

In any event using either the NIOSH method or referring to the Snook and Ciriello guidelines would lead you to the same conclusion, namely, that the task of unloading the pallets would be physically acceptable for most workers.

Having completed the depalletizing task, the attention now focuses on analyzing the loading of stock onto conveyors via the loading chutes.

Lift: Shelf to Loading Chute

The NIOSH analysis of this task is complicated by the fact that H is variable. H is influenced by the rotation of the carton and probably affected by the presence of an obtrusive shelf. H is half of 17″, rather than half of 15″ as in the first task. Cartons are lifted horizontally and moved ahead slightly to bring them to rest on the edge of the loading surface. To account for forward shift 2″ is arbitrarily added to give a more realistic approximation of the lift. The calculation is as follows:

H = at the origin: $(17″/2) + 6″ = 14.5″$ (36 cm)
at the destination: add 2″ = $14.5″ + 2″ = 16.5″$ (41 cm)

V = 30″ shelf height − 5″ platform = 25″ (62 cm)

D = 47″ loading chute height − 30″ shelf height
= 17″ (42.5 cm) corrected for platform. D also increases by approximately 1″ when the carton is rotated

F = 1.2 to 1.5 lifts/min, as before

From the NIOSH guidelines, these calculations yield discounting factors as follows:

$$\mathbf{H} = 0.36 \text{ to } 0.41 \quad \mathbf{V} = 0.95 \qquad \mathbf{D} = 0.88 \qquad \mathbf{F} = 0.89$$

Thus, the NIOSH **Action Limit,** that is, the level at which some intervention is required, is as follows:

$$
\begin{aligned}
\mathbf{AL} \text{ (lb)} \quad &= 90(0.36)(0.95)(0.88)(0.89) \\
&= 24 \,(11 \text{ kg})
\end{aligned}
$$

The average weight of a carton (22 lb or 10 kg), therefore, does not exceed the weight limit for the *ideal* lift, but practically speaking the two are ostensibly the same. This particular lift involves a significant amount of asymmetric handling and bending, with some cartons heavier than others. Furthermore, as each carton is hoisted into position, it is rotated and moved forward. Neither of these circumstances is covered by the NIOSH guidelines, which refer to optimal lifting conditions that do not exist here. It can be concluded that the NIOSH limit represents the best case scenario, while the true limit has an indefinite value somewhat less. The Action Limit is similar to the limit given by Snook and Ciriello for females lifting at a frequency of one lift/minute.

As in the first lift, the greatest restriction to lifting is imposed by H, the horizontal reach factor. Thus, intervention would be best directed by addressing this specific factor. The shelf upon which the cartons are opened protrudes beyond the loading chute, but when cartons are rotated on to their sides the cartons are wider than the shelf. It can be deduced that workers are not forced to reach forward with the arms extended holding the load away from the body, because carton width, rather than shelf width, is the limiting condition. Reducing H, the width of the cartons, would all but correct this situation and provide for a greater margin of acceptability. This might be easier said than done, however, since the cartons are used elsewhere in the process for the final packaging and shipment of goods.

From the foregoing results you would be hard pressed to convince an unreceptive management of the necessity for intervention on the basis of weight handling alone. Action Limits are not exceeded though some further compensatory reductions could be argued, because the lifting postures and demands are clearly less than ideal.

The analysis is not quite complete, however. While individually each task appears to be within acceptable limits, an integrated assessment of the overall physical demands remains to be established. A composite analysis of lifts one and two, similar to that previously done, is shown below:

Collective Analysis of Lifts 1 and 2

H (avg) = 13.5″ + 16.5″ / 2 = 15″ (38 cm)

V (avg) = 25″ (62 cm)

D (avg) = 25″ + 17″/2 = 21″ (52 cm)

F (cum) = 1.5 + 1.5 = 3 lifts/min

Using these parameters to calculate the devaluation of the limit yields:

H = 0.4	**V** = 0.95	**D** = 0.85	**F** = 0.75, and
AL (lb)	= 90(0.4)(0.95)(0.85)(0.75)		
	= 21.8 lb (9.7 kg)		

Virtually the same results are found using the data of Snook and Ciriello.

Analyses, then, point to the likelihood that the physical demands of the job are adding to the intemperate attitudes, though they are unlikely to be the cause. A pragmatist would argue that the simple interventions represent a win-win situation for the employer and the employees alike. They are feasible to implement without substantive changes to the process and are not likely to require a large financial commitment at this time. If for no other reason, basic modifications to the materials handling technique will allow a larger volume of materials to be handled, while reducing both the incidence of damage and the physical demands. The benefits of doing so seem quite clear.

RECOMMENDATIONS

Other than infeasible modifications of the weight and bulk of the containers and the nature of the manual handling process, some very practical and easy-to-implement changes might be suggested.

Elimination of the shelf

The shelf was probably introduced to facilitate opening of the cartons, although, in fact, all it does is compound the problem. A small table at one side of the loading chute would serve the same purpose and make it easier to load cartons on to the loading chute. This might improve the situation somewhat, but problems would still arise from the need for repetitive twisting of the body. Simply placing the pallet to one side near the loading chute might achieve a similar effect allowing cartons to be opened prior to unloading.

Condense two lifts into one

The two lifts would be condensed into one, simplifying the lifting and making it easier, if the pallets were strategically placed near the loading chute. Cartons could be opened and rotated before lifting them from the pallet. It is difficult to envisage that open flaps would interfere with handling any more than they do at this time.

Use boxes with removable lids

It may be possible to use boxes with removable lids instead of flaps. The current process caters to the sorting and re-packaging function, which explains why the cartons are positioned and opened as they are. This option would circumvent a major problem, but would require more investigation because of the potential impact on other operations in the packaging and production area.

Improve design and layout of work station

The difficulties of manual handling might be substantially alleviated by an improved design and layout of the work station, bearing in mind that, in fact, reduction and prevention of damage are the sole stated objectives of the review. Spillage might be reduced, for example, by providing guide rails to help position the cartons and dividers to create pigeonholes for holding the contents of the cartons as they are turned. The loading chute is at an awkward height for manipulating and transferring the cartons. The chute could readily be relocated at waist height without further need for a standing platform, hence also eliminating the hazard of tripping. Workers are required to step up as they carry the cartons to the loading chute. By routine they have come to know of its existence and avoid falls. This strategy of avoidance may in fact influence the manner in which cartons are carried, but at the same time make the process more awkward than is necessary.

Provide better handholds

The existing handholds for the cartons are too small and indeed can cause soft tissue damage to the fingers. Larger, more accessible handholds would assist the handling.

Job assignment and rotation

Where permissible, with due concern for union agreements and human rights guidelines or legislation, arrangements could be made to assign stronger workers (male and female) to the job.

Mechanically sophisticated modifications

Other more sophisticated mechanical improvements might include the following. Firstly, the lifting distance could be minimized by placing the pallets on to a self-adjusting platform which would eliminate stooping as the pallet is depleted. Secondly, rather than having multiple loading chutes, a short pivoting conveyor section could be devised to direct the flow of goods, as is used, for example, by cashiers at supermarket checkouts.

Case III

THE SCRUBBERS' SCOURGE

A company producing seat cushions for the automotive industry has received a number of complaints from its employees regarding shoulder aches and sore arms, some of which have led to sickness absenteeism and workers' compensation claims. The plant employs nearly 150 persons, mostly female, typically between the ages of 26 and 34. Preliminary investigation has shown that problems have arisen among a group of employees working at an injection molding operation which produces foam seat cushions for automobiles. Workers are required, among other things, to repeatedly clean the molds after each cycle. The cleaning procedure is thought to be the most likely cause of the problems, since there is little else in the way of activity required of these workers. While cleaning may normally be considered relatively harmless work, except on such occasions where chemical exposure or entry into a confined space is likely, even cleaning has its unique problems. As a consultant ergonomist, you have been asked to make recommendations to alleviate the problem. The challenge is not to find the cause, which clearly derives from a requirement to work in awkward postures, but to find solutions which are practical. Here is some background information which may be helpful in solving the problems.

THE PROCESS

Injection molding is the best known and most widely used method of fabricating plastic modules. Originally, thermoplastic resins such as polyolefins and polystyrene were commonly used for the purpose, but more recently thermosetting plastics have come into common use. The process essentially comprises the injection of melted and/or foamed plastic into a tightly sealed mould. The plastic solidifies, taking the shape of the cavity of the mould. Almost any of the thermoplastics can also be blow moulded or extruded, depending upon the application and the design of the final product. Blow moulding, for example, tends to be

32

used for producing hollow or tubular objects such as containers and bottles for beverages, detergents, cosmetics, and so on.

High-density foam seat cushions are produced by injecting a chemical plastic mixture under pressure into the mold cavity. The injection nozzle causes an effervescence of the fluids with extensive formation of plastic bubbles resembling soap suds. The plastic sets before the majority of the bubbles collapse, resulting in a porous foam. Following injection, the contents of the mold are allowed to remain briefly *in situ* to cure and to allow for the heat to be dissipated. The product is then removed and the process repeated in quick succession. In principle, the procedure is not that different from molding ceramics or metals, except for the use of chemical agents in the mix, such as stabilizers, curing agents and so on.

Equipment

Each mold is a stainless steel basin or cuvette with a fitted steel cover capable of sealing the cuvette. The mold is shallow, wide and long, with a contoured top (the lid) and bottom (the cuvette). The contours determine the final shape and thickness of the seat cushions. The cover is hinged at the rear, allowing it to swing open for cleaning. It opens to about 60° only and is restricted from further extension. The lid is also fastened to prevent escape and spillage of molten plastic during injection. The basin sits on legs with a minimum clearance height of 35 in (88 cm) from the floor when the top is opened for cleaning (Fig. III-1). A hose attached at an injection port provides the chemical feedstock for the injection of foam.

The molds are positioned to form continuous rows of 9–12 units (Fig. III-2), each unit separated from the next by only a few inches. The layout affords no room between units to allow for maneuvering. Work is performed from a standing position in front of the unit, with each operator tending three units. The floor is concrete, but rubber mats are provided to help reduce fatigue. No other tools or equipment are used during production except for conveyor belts that transport cushions to other work stations for upholstering, bracing, finishing and so on. The conveyor belts are located behind the operator.

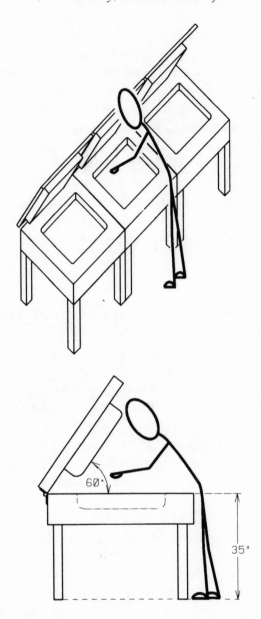

Figure III-1. A schematic of the relevant dimensions and equipment features showing the cuvette of the mold with the lid fully extended.

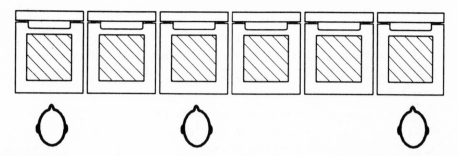

Figure III-2. A plan view of the layout showing a group of operators tending to a row of injection units abutted one against the other. This is a partial layout of one row, whereas there are typically nine to twelve units in a row, and several rows of similar equipment in the plant.

Working Conditions

By most industrial standards working conditions at the plant are quite acceptable. Compared with other sister manufacturing facilities in this automotive family, labor relations are more cordial and the atmosphere less tense. Though the work is not particularly interesting, the pay, the hours, and the benefits are satisfactory. As members of a major automotive trade union, the workers are generally well paid. At the present, wages are even slightly better than the norm because of a recent contract settlement. A sign outside the employee entrance indicates that the previous lost-time accident was 78 days ago. Noise levels inside range from 87 to 92 dBA throughout the plant. In the injection moulding area the sound pressure levels are all above 90 dBA. The wearing of protective earplugs is enforced. Temperatures are usually on the warm side because of the heat generated during the process, but heat stress is not a problem.

The Task

The operator's job is to ensure that the process runs smoothly and that the equipment functions properly. The injection phase is operator controlled, but semiautomated. It requires little skill. During injection, the operator's role is largely one of monitoring. After the foam has cooled and set, the cushions are manually removed from the mold and placed on the conveyor belt behind the worker. Their removal and stacking requires relatively little effort, but while the process is not machine-paced there are minimum production standards to be met. The pace must be kept brisk. After a cushion has been removed from the mold the cavity is then cleaned by scrubbing. Wax is intermittently applied by the operator to the inner surfaces of the mold to help prevent sticking and to minimize the amount of cleaning.

The work cycle thus consists of the following steps: securing the lid, injecting the polymer, allowing for curing, removing the molded cushions, cleaning the residues from the inner surfaces of the molds and occasionally applying wax. The cycle time comprises approximately two-thirds machine time and one-third operator time. Injection and curing determine the machine time. The operator's time, however, is largely spent in cleaning off pieces of foam adhered to the surfaces. Scrubbing is done with abrasive pads, not unlike those commonly available for household cleaning chores. Work quotas leave little time to struggle with the stubborn residual fragments that seem to bind firmly and refuse to surrender.

Scrubbing

During scrubbing the operator is required to make long extended reaches in awkward postures to remove residues and adherent fragments. Often a simple reach is inadequate to access the distant areas in the cavity even with the arm fully outstretched. Thus, and particularly with workers of small stature, it is common to find an operator bent well forward into the mold cavity, the upper torso involved in a contortionist's exercise, the midsection pressed against an edge of the basin, the knees hyperextended, and the leg muscles stretched to their limits. Sometimes one leg is lifted, while the other is planted on tiptoes if need be, to make long extended reaches (Fig. III-3).

From the amount of time that workers spend at this activity you can appreciate why there are complaints related to working postures. You might even suspect that there are other problems equally as unpleasant which have gone unnoticed or at least remain largely unreported, such as overextension of the knee, or repetitive strain injury in the operative wrist and hand. There is also a host of other problems of lesser significance, including cuts and abrasions to the forearms and elbows from scraping against the molds. Cushion handling is not a major problem despite the awkward size since the cushions are light in weight and are moved with ease. Occasionally, an operator might, with little or no effect, bump a forearm or jar an elbow while handling a cushion.

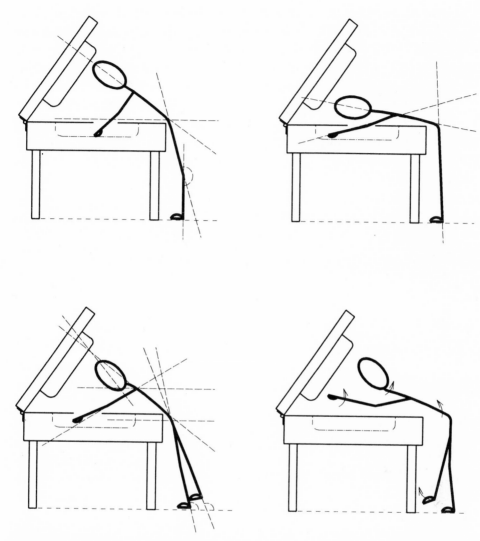

Figure III-3. A schematic showing the awkward reaches and postures encountered in the scrubbing task. Literally every joint is at one time or another bent, twisted, rotated, and/or extended to extremes of motion. At times the operator is forced to lean into the belly of the mold and to stand on one foot to perform long extended reaches.

ASSIGNMENT

Even without knowing any of the particulars relating to dimensions, reaches, and so on, you should be able to make recommendations on ways of improving the working conditions in this particular plant, if not in detail then certainly in principle. There are different strategies for dealing with the problems. Some may include administrative approaches, such as job rotation, added or increased rest pauses, hand and torso exercises, and so on. Some may offer a partial solution only. Some may be easier to implement and better suited than others. For the moment, consider only engineering/ergonomic approaches, bearing in mind that management will not look favorably on costly solutions. Keep in mind also that the client may have limitations you are unaware of. Offer a range of suggestions on how to modify/redesign the equipment and layout, assuming that practical constraints exist. Costs rule out comprehensive design changes.

THE SCRUBBERS' SCOURGE SOLUTION

In attempting a solution, one should consider some or all of the following principles:

- minimize reach distances
- provide better tools for cleaning
- improve access to the mold
- modify the design/equipment as appropriate
- change the process as appropriate

The strategies of choice will depend on your client's ability to implement them, as well as cost effectiveness and willingness to follow through. Improvements you might suggest include the following:

1. Change of workplace layout to make the equipment more accessible and scrubbing easier, assuming that space is available. Simply by spacing the molding injection units further apart to allow for movement between them would improve accessibility to the units, eliminating some of the long and awkward reaches.

2. Tilt the units forward by changing the height of the front and rear leg supports. This would facilitate unloading and cleaning if the lid was fully extendable, rather than restricted. Alternatively, the lid might be hinged to one side. In either case, cleaning the underside of the lid would be easier and more space would be available for working. If tilting creates problems for the product, the basin and lid could be tilted for cleaning after the formative process.

3. Removal of the cover for cleaning, as an alternative to a more fully extendable lid, or to side fastening, would allow considerably better access than the present hinge arrangement, particularly if there was freedom to move around the units from front to rear and from side to side. Cleaning the covers after removal would also be easier, although more time might be needed to reposition and fix the lid.

4. The lip which aligns the cover and basin, if removed, relocated or replaced, would help to prevent elbow and forearm injuries and to

minimize local compression on the soft tissues of the abdomen or chest while leaning inwards. For these reasons, it is better on the cover rather than on the basin. Adding a rubber sheath might provide some further protection if none of the above are acceptable.

5. A scrubbing tool with a handle would reduce the need for extended reaches. The tool could be either manually operated or power driven, in the form of a simple lightweight brush with a firm handle, or a set of rotating brushes, or whatever configuration might seem appropriate. Weight would almost certainly be a factor for any power tool, however, unless the bulk of the weight were supported on a retractable support.

6. More frequent inspection of the condition of the mold would help in identifying damaged surfaces which tend to promote adhesion and increase the need for cleaning. Excessive scrubbing, in turn, removes the previously applied waxy film and promotes adhesion. Thus, once the surface is impaired a feedback cycle is initiated, more scrubbing is needed, and the more scrubbing the greater the likelihood of adhesions, the greater the adhesion the more scrubbing needed, and so on.

7. A simple change of process such as use of a better wax, or waxing before each cycle, could eliminate much of the problem, assuming that an appropriate (spray) wax could be found.

8. Use of a cleaning agent that dissolves residues would significantly reduce the labor of scrubbing and might simplify the task to one of wiping down the surfaces. A number of chemical agents can be found to dissolve foam.

9. Coating the mold surfaces with a non-adherent covering such as Teflon, or some other non-stick material, could reduce or even eliminate the need for scrubbing.

The foregoing recommendations are not necessarily all of the suggestions that could be implemented. Each, however, could be considered on its merits, along with others that you might think of, and could be put into effect as and when feasible, depending on such considerations as cost, space availability, engineering feasibility and so on, which are not considered here at this time.

Case IV

THE ANNEALER'S ANATHEMA

BACKGROUND

Magnesium alloy car rims (also known as wheel hubs, wheel centers, sports rims, mag wheels) are shipped to this heat treating facility for annealing, a process which renders them more durable. The rims are removed from their shipping bins, stamped and processed, then placed in the original bins for return to the supplier. The work is physical, steady, uneventful, but the pay is good. The manager who is the owner, operator and boss says that workers are not bothered by back pain. He says the workers do as they are told and they don't complain. The fact that he is highly unapproachable may have something to do with this. He grumbles that they have nothing to complain about and that "they get paid well for the kind of work they do." If there is any complaining to do, he feels that he is the only one with cause. His major complaint is turnover and he cannot understand why. He cannot seem to keep furnace operators for more than a few months. Most of the workers in the plant have come from an immigrant population. Records are nonexistent.

The Process

Magnesium alloy rims arrive at the shipping/receiving dock in metal crates or tote bins, each tote containing eighteen rims of the "green" unprocessed stock. The tote bins are transported by forklift to an operator who unloads the "green" stock, embosses each rim with a batch identification number, and loads the rims onto racks for heat treating. Racks are filled to capacity (eighteen wheel rims), then hoisted into a furnace two at a time. Annealing takes slightly longer than one hour, after which the racks are shunted to a second furnace for an equivalent period of time. The rims are withdrawn, cooled, then re-loaded into the original totes for shipment. The process is illustrated in Figures IV-1 through IV-4.

41

Figure IV-1. Wheel rims are shipped in metal tote bins for annealing. The rims are stacked loosely in the bins in three layers of six rims, each layer separated by a thick piece of cardboard to prevent damage during shipment. In the background several empty spindle racks are visible. Rims are taken from the bins and placed on to the spindles of the racks after being embossed with identification numbers.

Tools and Equipment

Each tote bin is filled with eighteen rims, stacked in three layers of six rims. The rims lie flat on their sides and are loosely stacked allowing for some minor shifting during shipment. Pieces of cardboard or plywood separate the layers to prevent damage during shipping. The dimensions of the tote bin are 44″ wide, 55″ long and 38″ high. One of the long sides is hinged midway allowing the top half to fold down. This is to facilitate loading and unloading of the rims but is seldom, if ever, taken advantage of. Fully loaded, each bin weighs approximately 800 lbs. A manually operated, manually powered forklift is used to maneuver tote bins for more convenient positioning during emptying and reloading (Fig. IV-1).

Each treating racks consists of six upright spindles mounted on a metal base (see Fig. IV-1). The spindles function as spines for stacking the rims. The hub of the wheel rim is open, allowing the spindle to slide through the center as the rim is lowered on to it. Rims are stacked three deep on one of six spindles with spacers between for distribution of heat

Figure IV-2. The operator in this photo is unloading a rim from one of the tote bins. Notice the stooped posture during unloading. Extended reaches are sometimes necessary, particularly as the bin approaches emptiness. In the background, part of a furnace is seen off to the right and off to the left is a heat treating rack full of rims.

(Fig. IV-4). Each rack holds eighteen rims. Racks are designed to hold the same number of rims as the tote bins.

Racks are stacked and heat treated two at a time, the stack having a combined height of 66" and a combined weight of approximately 1500 lbs. Loaded racks are transferred to and from the furnaces by using an overhead hydraulic hoist. The power hoist is used for transferring racks to and from the furnaces. At one time it was also used to shift the racks from one furnace to the other during the heat treating process, but a short conveyor section was recently installed allowing the racks to be automatically shifted between the furnaces.

Embossing is done manually with a mallet and stylus. The mallet is 12" long and weighs approximately 11 lbs. It has a solid copper head and a hollow metal handle. The stylus resembles a cold chisel weighing 2–3 lbs (Fig. IV-3).

Rims are made of a magnesium-aluminum alloy (Fig. IV-3). They weigh 35 lbs, are 8" deep, and have a diameter of 13", although there is some variation in size, style and weight from one automobile manufacturer to the next.

Figure IV-3. Wheel rims are embossed using a hammer and stylus before undergoing annealing. The stylus resembles a cold chisel and weighs about 2–3 lbs. The hammer, not shown here, weighs nearly 11 lbs.

The Task

The furnace operator single-handedly performs all of the above-mentioned tasks of manual materials handling, embossing, and furnace tending. Except for the dolly and overhead hoist, all work is performed unassisted. To begin, the operator moves one, or sometimes two, bins of "green stock" from a temporary storage area to a more convenient site nearer to his workbench and the furnaces. This is done manually (Fig. IV-1), because the hoist does not have sufficient reach. Starting from the most accessible and working towards the least accessible, rims are removed one at a time from the bin and placed on the workbench. Each rim is stamped with an identification number by striking the stylus and leaving an imprint on the metal. This is done for quality control purposes to keep track of each batch. After embossing, the rim is transferred from the bench to an adjacent spot on the floor where the rims are temporarily stockpiled (Fig. IV-5). A second rim is removed from the bin, stamped, placed on the floor; then a third; and so on, until the tote is empty and the rims are piled two and three high on the

Figure IV-4. After embossing, the rims are eventually loaded on to heat treating racks. Two racks are stacked one on top of the other before being shunted to the furnace. A chain, part of the grapple for hoisting the racks, is seen dangling in the center of the photo.

floor. An empty heat treating rack is then located and loaded with the stamped rims.

After filling the first rack, a second rack is placed on top of the first and is loaded with rims. Two racks are always stacked together allowing 36 rims to be processed simultaneously. While some rims are being heat treated, others are being prepared and still others are cooling and being readied for shipment. One operator performs all of the manual handling; loading, unloading and transfer. Most effort and time are spent in unloading and loading either the "green stock" or the annealed rims. Activities are interrupted briefly to tend the furnaces. When the heating cycle is complete, racks are removed from the furnace, making room available for two more.

Unloading the racks is simply the process of loading done in reverse. Rims are unloaded by lifting them over the top of the spindles and returning them to the tote bins for shipment. As time permits, the finished rims are manually transferred to a temporary holding area, to be subsequently collected by the personnel from shipping.

Figure IV-5. Rims are processed in batches, typically one bin at a time. The rims are embossed then stockpiled on the floor until the bin is emptied, at which point the stockpile is depleted to fill the heat treating racks. Up to three rims are stacked on top of each other on the floor.

Volume and Pace of Work

Fourteen bins of "green stock" are processed during each 8-hour work shift. To minimize downtime, the flow of rims is maintained during shift changes and breaks. Heat treating continues. Generally, there are racks of annealed parts to be unloaded, or *greenware* to be loaded when the end of the shift arrives. The incoming operator simply picks up the work where the other left off.

In total, approximately thirty-five minutes of operator time is spent during the first phase of preparation, namely, stamping and loading of the parts on to the racks. Half as much time is spent in unloading the heat treated parts, the difference being attributed to the identification and stamping. The remainder of the time is divided between furnace tending and maneuvering bins, racks, tools and/or parts. Work is steady without opportunity for prolonged pauses.

Layout

The present layout is largely dictated by the flow of work. Space is not a constraint. There is plenty of unused, open floor space creating a tendency for the equipment to sprawl. The arrangement of equipment is rather haphazard as shown in Figure IV-6. Except for the furnaces, the equipment can be easily rearranged.

The Workers

Currently, the job is held by young males, all under the age of thirty-four. A twenty-seven-year-old male, 5'9" tall, 170 lbs was seen working at the time of your visit. He is strong, healthy and has no health complaints. He assumed this job approximately 6 months ago after the previous occupant left the company. The other regulars have been on the job for only a short time. They have not expressed any complaints about their job. Specific details about these individuals are lacking.

Physical Demands

Furnace operator is a slight misnomer, because the job largely involves manual handling of parts, more so than furnace tending. Lifting, carrying, positioning and lowering of rims occupy the majority of the activity. Each rim is handled on four separate occasions. A summary of the manual handling requirements is given in Figure IV-7. Not included are the numerous instances where the operator is found pushing and pulling a load. These are comparatively minor physical demands within the scheme of things.

ASSIGNMENT

With the information you have been given about the facility and the particulars related to the job you are required to show that the manual handling tasks are likely to pose a risk to the furnace operator. Specifically, you should:

(1) Assess the physical demands of the job. Calculate the NIOSH lifting limits as discussed in Case 2 and outlined in Appendix 2. Compare your results with the recommendations of Snook and Ciriello as indicated in Appendix 3. Comment on the physical demands for

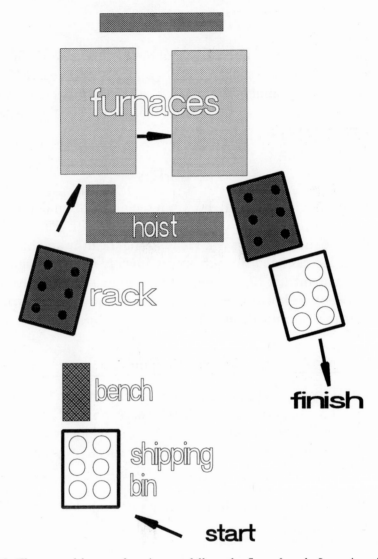

Figure IV-6. The general layout of equipment follows the flow of work. Incoming rims are placed adjacent to the workbench for embossing. Once embossed, they are eventually, although not directly, loaded on to the racks for annealing. Annealed rims cool after being removed from the furnaces and are re-loaded into bins for shipment. The operator is positioned in the central area amid all of the equipment.

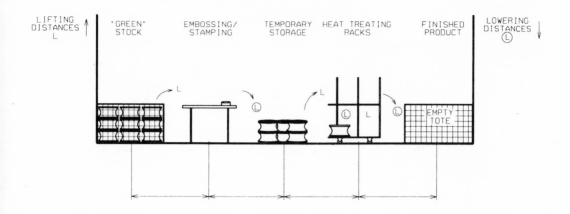

Figure IV-7. A summary of the furnace operator's work showing the four stages of manual handling, some of which involve lifting, others of which involve lowering and all of which involve carrying. The origins and destinations of each transfer are sketched. Distances are given in Table IV-1.

carrying and lowering, with reference to the Snook and Ciriello guidelines.

(2) Make recommendations on how to redesign the task to alleviate the burden of manual labor.

(3) As an aside, you may wish to note the proposed revisions to the NIOSH equation that are under consideration. Further details appear in Appendix 2.

In making your calculations use a piecewise approach. Calculate the NIOSH lifting limits for each individual task identified in Figure IV-7. In sequential order the tasks may be described as:

- lift rim from bin; carry to table
- emboss rim; carry to stockpile; lower to floor or stack
- lift rim from stockpile, carry to rack, load on to rack
- lift rim from rack; carry; place in bin for shipping.

Develop an integrated assessment of the job as a whole taking into account the multiple lifting components and the other aspects of the job. Use the measurements given in Table IV–I for estimating the vertical and horizontal displacement factors in the NIOSH equation.

For calculation purposes and in accordance with the NIOSH guidelines make an idealistic assumption that the operator always uses symmetrical, two-handed lifts, grabbing the top of the rim at the perimeter.

Table IV-1
DIMENSIONS ASSOCIATED WITH EACH TASK,
A VIEW FROM THE OPERATOR'S PERSPECTIVE

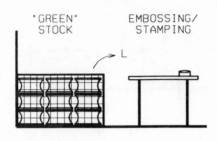

3 <u>layers</u> of greenstock in bins, each separated by cardboard: rims *rest* at heights of 3", 11" and 21" above floor.

<u>Two reach distances</u> for unloading: *nearby* rims are 12.5" from the side to midpoint of rim; *far* rims are 31.5" from the same side (not shown).

<u>Bench</u> height is 42".

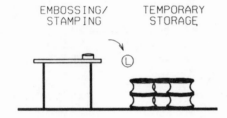

Greenware <u>stock-piled</u> 3 high on the floor at 0", 8" and 16" (rim base).

<u>Bench</u> height, as shown above.

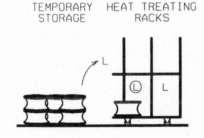

Rims (base) seated on to <u>2 racks</u>: *lower rack* at 5", 15" and 25" (Fig. IV-IX); *upper rack* at 38", 48", 58".

<u>Stock-pile</u>, as indicated above.

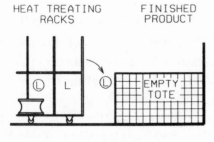

Destination of the annealed rims in the bins, as shown in the first task.

Origin of lift from the racks based on the dimensions given above

TASK   **DIMENSIONS**

Most often, rims are handled this way, although there are some exceptions. The rims lie flat in the tote bins, on the workbench, or on the racks. Whether they lie face up or face down is of no consequence.

As you begin to calculate the NIOSH limits for the first lift you will undoubtedly notice that H, measured strictly by the position of the rim, is greater than or equal to H_{max}, for rims furthest from the operator, namely, those on the far side of the bin. In other words, the reach distances are too long, exceeding the normal range (H < 30") for lifting and reaching. Half the rims belong in this category. To overcome this problem and to reduce the lifting stress, the worker leans over the side of the bin (Fig. IV-2), grabs the rim with one hand, drags it closer to the body, and then lifts. The lifts are always made from the same side of the bin, namely, the side facing the workbench. This is an interesting point, because the annealed rims are reloaded into bins from each side, presumably because excessive reaches do not permit the rims to be easily placed.

The H factor used in this lift is, therefore, not the H distance measured between the body and the original position of the rim, but a smaller value. The appropriate H value is the new position of the rim, from which the lift is initiated. By setting $H = H_{max}$ you would overestimate the stress. The H dimension is actually variable and is influenced by the way the operator leans forward to reach the rim, how far he leans and at what angle. Whether the operator lifts from the upper, middle or bottom tier determines the posture and, in turn, sets the parameters of the H and V variables. Both H and V interact through the posture as illustrated in Figure IV-8. H is greatest at the top layer when the operator stretches ahead to lift and retract the rims and is smaller when the operator is fully stooped lifting rims from above.

To make reasonable approximations, assume the operator pulls the top rims six inches closer before lifting them with a jerk, reducing the forward reach dimension to 25" (Fig. IV-9). Assume the same dimension holds for the middle tier. For the bottom layer, the operator removes the closest rims first, then drags the others closer, placing them in more or less the same position before lifting. Thus, for determining the H factor of the bottom layer assume a forward reach dimension of 12" at the origin of the lift (Fig. IV-9), and also at the destination when reloading the bins for shipment.

For subsequent calculations of task 3 you will also need to know the configuration of the heat treating racks. Assume the spindles vis-á-vis the heat treating racks are spaced to produce a spatial arrangement that

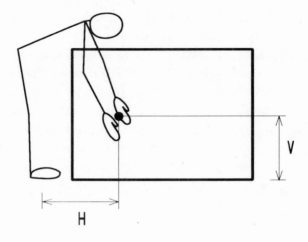

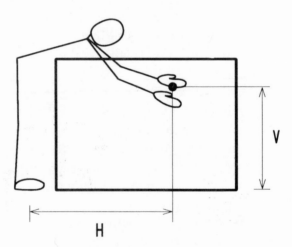

Figure IV-8. This illustration contrasts two different lifts performed during unloading of the bins to show the extent of variation within this single task. The factors H and V are determined by the position of the rim at the origin of the lift. As H and V differ, so do the lifting limits, which cautions against oversimplification of the analysis. A reasonable approximation of the task demands is needed, without understating the role of the critical elements. In this example, stooping to remove a rim from the bottom of a nearly empty bin may cause H to be small and V large, whereas when the bin is nearly full and the operator reaches ahead, H may be large and V small.

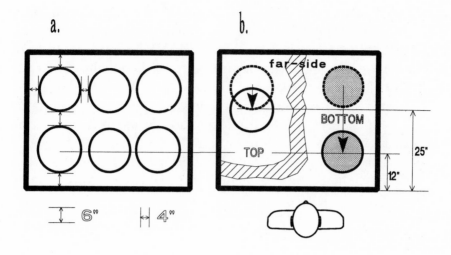

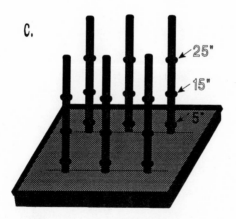

Figure IV-9. (a) Rims are jostled about during shipment, but for the purposes of calculation assume they arrive evenly spaced. The arrangement of one such layer is shown. (b) The H factor is influenced by the reach requirements. For rims on the near side of the bin, reach is not a problem. But to reduce the lifting stress, the rims at the far side of the bin are dragged closer to the operator before the lift is initiated. For calculation, assume the operator drags the rims 6 inches closer when removing the top layer. For the bottom layer, the far rims are dragged even closer as shown. (c) Rims are stacked on to the spindles of heat treating racks and are seated at three different heights: 5, 15 and 25 inches, respectively. The top of the spindles is 33 inches above the floor. A second rack is stacked on top (not shown).

matches the positioning of the rims in the tote bins (dimensions shown in Table IV–I and Fig. IV-9). This is a fairly accurate depiction as you might be able to ascertain from Figure IV-1. The implication of this is that H will be the same, whether lifting from the tote bins or removing rims from the spindle racks.

Mistakenly you may overlook a few details without significantly changing the results such as forgetting to factor in an inch or two for the cardboard separators in the bins or forgetting to factor in the thickness of the base. For accuracy the details have been included in the solutions. Your objective should be to provide a reasonably close approximation.

THE ANNEALER'S ANATHEMA SOLUTION

You have already seen in Case II how to apply the NIOSH formula to a relatively simple problem. This case presents a much more complex application using the same principles.

As a point of interest your quick mental exercise should have indicated that a total of 35,000 pounds is manually handled (lifted, carried, lowered) each shift. This estimate was derived in the following manner. There are fourteen totes of *green* stock, or 252 rims processed each shift. Each rim is handled four times amounting to the equivalent of approximately 1000 lifts/shift accompanied by as many incidents of carrying and lowering. Thus, 35 lbs/lift × 1000 lifts/shift amounts to 35,000 lbs handled during one shift, a surprisingly high value.

For comparison, assuming all lifting conditions are ideal, that is, the load is always lifted close to the body, the vertical height at the start of the lift is equal to 30″, the lifting distance does not exceed 10″, that lifting is evenly distributed over the work shift, yielding an average frequency of two lifts per minute, with no discounting for H, V, or D, then NIOSH guidelines, in fact, would allow for approximately 35,000 kg to be lifted, an amount of astonishing proportions, twice the value computed for this work. Using the information derived from Appendix 2 and Case II this can be shown as follows:

$$
\begin{aligned}
AL\,(lbs) \ &= 90\,(HF)(VF)(DF)(FF) \\
&= 90\,(1)\,(1)\,(1)\,(.85) \\
&= 75\,(35\ kg) \qquad FF\ obtained\ from\ graph
\end{aligned}
$$

Thus, under optimal circumstances NIOSH would permit a lift twice the amount currently being handled. However, none of the lifting conditions is ideal, and if you analyze each component of the lift separately you obtain considerably more restrictive lifting limits, as shown in the following detailed calculations.

DETAILED CALCULATIONS

Task 1—Unloading Tote Bins

As many as six points of origin are needed to arrive at a precise assessment, because H and V both vary depending upon the position of the rim in the tote bin (Fig. IV-8). Performing the NIOSH calculations in logical sequence, that is the order in which the rims are removed from the bin, yields the following set of calculations:

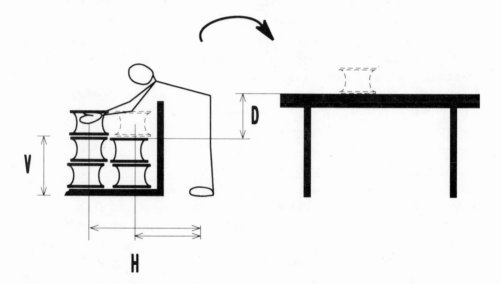

Figure IV-10. The lifting factors associated with unloading of the rims are illustrated, the details of which appear in the text. D may be measured from either the top of the rim (position of the grip) or the bottom, but must be consistent. The F factor is not illustrated.

Upper Layer (lifting factors illustrated in Fig. IV-10)

    H has 2 values:
    far-side   = 25″ (reach) + 6″ (body interference)
                = 31″ (77.5 cm)
    near-side = 12″ (reach) + 6″ (body interference)
                = 18″ (45 cm)

    V = thickness of 3 layers + thickness of base + spacers
      = 3 × 8″ (rim depth) + 3″ (base of bin) + 2 × 1″ (cardboard separators)
      = 29″ (72.5 cm) position of the grip

D = destination − origin

   = bench top − base of the rim

   = 42″ (bench height) − 29″ (point of grip) − 8″ (rim depth)

   = 21″ (52.5 cm) travel

F = number of lifts/lifting interval(s)

   number of lifts: 14 bins × 18 rims/bin

                = 252 lifts/3 layers of rims

                = 84 rims/layer

   near-side = 84/2 lifts = 42 lifts

   far side   = same

   total time = 7 intervals × 35 min/interval = 225 min

   = 42 lifts/225 min. for each side

   = 0.2 lift/min for each H, or 1 lift every 5 min

          yielding, discounting factors of

near side   HF = 0.33   VF = 0.99   DF = 0.84   FF = 0.98

far side   HF = 0.19   VF, DF, FF are the same

      NIOSH Action Limits, then, are as follows:

AL (lb)   = 90(*HF* above)(.99)(.84)(.98)

           = 24.2 (11 kg) on the *near side* of the bin

           = 14.1 (6.4 kg) on the *far side* of the bin

Middle Layer

H = same two values as shown above

V = thickness of 2 layers + thickness of base + spacer

   = 2 × 8″ (rim depth) + 3″ (base of bin) + 1″ (cardboard separator)

   = = 20″ (50 cm) position of the grip

D = destination − origin

   = bench top − base of the rim

   = 42″ (bench height) − 20″ (point of grip) − 8″ (rim depth)

   = 30″ (75 cm) travel

F = 0.2 lift/min, as above

          yielding, discounting factors of

HF = .33 and .19   VF = .9   DF = .8   FF = .98

NIOSH Action Limit:

AL (lb) $= 90(HF$ above$)(.9)(.8)(.98)$
$= 21.0$ (9.5 kg) on the near side
$= 12.1$ (5.5 kg) on the far side

Bottom Layer

H has only one value as shown in Figure IV-9
$= 12'' + 6'' = 18''$ (45 cm)

V $=$ thickness of 1 layer $+$ thickness of the base
$= 8''$ (rim depth) $+ 3''$ (base of bin)
$= 11''$ (27.5) position of the grip

D $=$ destination $-$ origin
$= 42''$ (bench height) $- 11''$ (point of grip) $= 8''$ (rim depth)
$= 39''$ (97.5 cm) travel

F $= 0.4$ lift/min, twice the above because H is not subdivided

yielding, discounting factors of

HF $= .33$ VF $= .81$ DF $= .78$ FF $= .97$

NIOSH Action Limit:

AL (lb) $= 90(.33)(.81)(.78)(.97)$
$= 18.2$ (8.3 kg)

Composite average for this task is derived as follows:

H (avg) $= [4(18) + 2(31)]/6 = 22.3''$ (56 cm)

V (avg) $= [29 + 20 + 11]/3 = 20''$ (50 cm)

D (avg) $= [21 + 30 + 39]/3 = 30''$ (75 cm)

F (cum) $= 252$ rims/225 min. $= 1.1$ lift/min

yielding, discounting factors of

HF $= .27$ VF $= .9$ DF $= .8$ FF $= .91$

NIOSH Action Limit:

AL (lb) $= 90(.27)(.9)(.8)(.91)$
$= 15.9$ (7.2 kg)

NIOSH guidelines in these circumstances would recommend that the upper limit (Maximum Permissible Limit $= 3 \times$ AL) not exceed 47.7 lbs (21.7 kg), which it does not. However, the Action Limit is exceeded by a significant margin in every one of the foregoing lifting positions. The Action Limits range from approximately thirteen to nineteen pounds, but the rims weigh twice this amount. Snook and Ciriello offer more liberal limits. Their closest approximation for the *average* task is given by the value of the maximum acceptable weight of lift for the 90th percentile male in the lifting range from floor to knuckle height (see Appendix 3). Using their *width* criterion (the counterpart to the NIOSH H factor) of 49 cm, their *distance* value (equivalent to the NIOSH D factor) of 76 cm the limit of 13 kg is given. In either case both the NIOSH guidelines and Snook and Ciriello limits are exceeded. You conclude that intervention is warranted, even if you neglect the attribution from carrying. If you factor into consideration that carrying adds to the physical demands of this task, your conclusions are all the more unequivocal.

Task 2—Stockpiling Rims on the Floor

Rims are carried from the workbench and lowered to a stockpile on the floor (Fig. IV-7). These activities comprise the second task of the furnace operator. Both activities place significant physical demands upon the operator that are not covered by the NIOSH formula. Ignore the carrying component for the moment. Let us explore the use of the NIOSH formula to establish upper limits for the lowering activity. Recall, it was previously argued in Case II that for lifting and lowering parameters which are otherwise similar, except for the directions of travel which are reversed, that is for reciprocal movements, the critical limit is determined by the lifting, not the lowering. This is borne out in the guidelines of Snook and Ciriello to which the reader is referred (App. 3).

Taking this into account leads to the possibility of a deriving a conservative estimate for the acceptable amount of lowering. The lowering/lifting factors are derived in the following manner. From Figure IV-5 it is determined that rims are stacked three high on the floor. This establishes the point of destination at three different heights and the *midpoint* of the stockpile as the average. Attempting to calculate the Action Limit for this lowering activity might lead to the following error:

$$H = H_{min}$$
$$= 6'' \, (10 \text{ cm}) \text{ i.e. rims held close to the body}$$

$\mathbf{V}$ = 42" (bench height) + 8" (rim depth)
= 50" (125 cm) point of grip

$\mathbf{D}$ = destination − origin
= midpoint of stockpile measured at the base of the rim − bench height
= 8" (rim depth) − 42" (bench height)
= −34" (85 cm) travel

$\mathbf{F}$ = 252 rims/3 tiers = 84 rims in the middle tier
= 84/225 min = .4 lifts(lowers)/min
NB. The appropriate F_{max} is for the stooped posture

yielding, discounting factors of

HF = 1	VF = .8	DF = .79	FF = .97

NIOSH Action Limits:

$\mathbf{AL}$ (lb) = 90(1)(.8)(.79)(.97)
= 55.2 (24.3 kg)

D, the travel distance, varies between 26" to 42", and is determined by the destination depending upon where the rims are placed in the stockpile, on top or on the floor, with .77 < DF < .81

$\mathbf{AL}$ varies accordingly, from 53.8 to 56.6 lb.

Composite Average for the task is determined by:

$\mathbf{H}$ and $\mathbf{V}$, as above

$\mathbf{D}_{avg}$ = D_{middle} = [26 + 34 + 42]/3 = −34" (85 cm)

$\mathbf{F}_{cum}$ = 252 lifts(lowers)/225 min.
= 1.1 lifts(lowers)/min.

yielding, discounting factors of

HF,VF,DF same   FF = .91

NIOSH Action Limit:

$\mathbf{AL}$ (lb) = 90(1)(.8)(.79)(.91)
= 51.8 (23.5 kg)

These NIOSH parameters describe a lowering activity, with an Action Limit calculated using the value of D and ignoring the sign. The rationale for this argues that distance is always a positive value; the sign merely indicates the direction of travel. This also makes the simplifying assumption that the physiological differences between lifting and lowering can be ignored. Assigning the absolute value to the D term does not take care of the problem, however. The intent is to describe an object being lowered to the floor from above waist height, but the result is quite different following the procedure outlined above. Literally, the description would fit that of a lift, commencing at approximately mid chest and ending at arm reach.

The formula was clearly not intended for the purpose of deriving guidelines for lowering. Thus arises the question of how to use the NIOSH method or whether to use it for estimating a guideline. Lifting from the floor to the workbench is opposite to the task of stockpiling rims. Calculating a *lifting* guideline for a *lowering* maneuver may, nevertheless, be helpful to determine an upper boundary. The Snook and Ciriello tables in Appendix 3 indicate that, consistently, lifting guidelines are more stringent than the corresponding guidelines for the opposite action of lowering between the same two points. Thus, the Action Limit for the countervailing lift determines an upper boundary for lowering, as well as lifting. While the limit may be imprecise and overly cautious in its recommendations, at least it provides a yardstick against which the task can be evaluated.

Calculation of the action limit for the countervailing lift, in this particular example results in minor differences only, because H and F factors stay the same as shown above: D is positive: V originates at 16″. Only the corresponding distance factor changes from 0.8 to 0.86, resulting in ostensibly the same outcome.

However, comparing the NIOSH results to Snook and Ciriello guidelines shows there are considerable differences between the two. Snook and Ciriello offer the following guidelines for males (90th percentile) lifting and lowering weights between floor and knuckle height. The task under discussion is within this approximate range. The maximum acceptable weights for lifting and lowering are 33 and 37 pounds (15 and 17 kg), respectively, assuming the center of mass is 13.5″ (34 cm) away from the body and the weight travels through a distance of 30″ (76 cm). Unfortunately, a closer approximation of the real task requires further interpolations, which are not possible from their data alone. The origins of this discrepancy are worth investigating, because the Snook and Ciriello guidelines suggest a task which hinges on the limits of acceptability, whereas NIOSH limits indicate a clearly acceptable task.

The NIOSH limits are highly sensitive to displacement of the load away from the body. During stockpiling the operator is able to hold the load next to the body, minimizing the effect of the H factor. Suppose this was not possible. What if the load was 13.5″ from the body as in the Snook and Ciriello tables? In this circumstance the NIOSH limit would be reduced by more than fifty percent. The H factor would diminish from a value of 1 to a 0.44 (Fig. IV-11), resulting in a recommended lifting limit of 24.5 lbs (11.1 kg), even more rigorous than the Snook and Ciriello guideline!

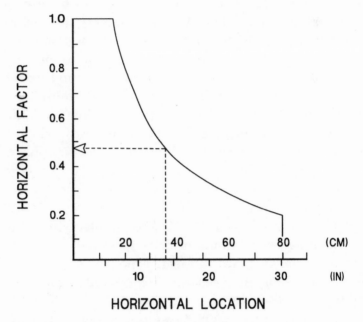

Figure IV-11. The discounting of the NIOSH lifting limit due to horizontal displacement of the load can be substantial. With an H location of 13.5 inches, the limit would be reduced by more than 50 percent.

From the preceding paragraph you may deduce that the NIOSH formula provides a more realistic approximation of the current task when faced with limited inferences from Snook and Ciriello. Thus, the action of lowering rims to the floor is, in and of itself, likely to be well within the range of acceptance.

Carrying of rims between locations is not covered by the NIOSH formula and has been neglected to this point. A cursory assessment is possible, however, by making reference to the guidelines of Snook and Ciriello. For a distance of 7–8 feet between the stockpile and the workbench a limit of 37 lbs (17 kg) is recommended by Snook and Ciriello. This is similar to their limit for lowering of rims from the workbench.

In a multiple component task involving lifting, lowering and/or carrying, the limit is best estimated by selecting the most critical element as the basis for a guideline. The lowering maneuver is not the critical element, but carrying may be. The limit for carrying, over the range of values covered by Snook and Ciriello, is not effected by the dimension of the load, except for extended horizontal reaches. Hence, the carrying limit for this task requires no further reevaluation.

For estimating the limits of a multiple task, therefore, each component is analyzed separately, using the frequency of the combined task. The combined frequency of 1.1 lowers/min plus 1.1 carries/min, in this case does not change the limits for carrying (App. 3), but does change the NIOSH lift limits. Even though the F factor in the NIOSH formula is reduced from 0.91 to 0.82 at the higher frequency, this has no effect on the guideline, because the carry is the critical element. Integrating both the carrying and lowering components leads to the conclusion that the task remains within reasonable expectations.

Load dimensions might be expected to influence carrying, but the Snook and Ciriello tables indicate a small effect, at least over the range of values they tested. The manner in which loads are usually carried, that is next to the body, is likely to be an important reason. This would effectively reduce H. Another factor might relate to postural accommodation. By arching backwards, the load can be more closely aligned with the center of gravity of the body, reducing the compressive forces on the spine.

Task 3—Loading the Heat Treating Racks

This is a multiple component manual handling task involving the transfer of rims between the stockpile and heat treating racks. Lifting, carrying and lowering of rims are all components of the task. Ignoring the carrying demands for the present, there are two other components to consider. The first is a lift from the floor, the second a lowering of rims onto the spindles of the heat treating racks.

Both the point of origin and the point of destination vary making this a complicated task. They vary depending upon the position of the rim in the stockpile and on the spindle. As in the previous calculation starting with the middle of the stockpile as the average point of origin allows for some simplification. The same can be done to calculate the average destination.

Heat treating racks are stacked two high. The bottom rack is filled taking the rims from the stockpile. Then, another empty rack is placed on top and filled. Rims are lifted to the top then lowered down on to the spindles. For calculating the lifting limit the height of the upper and lower spindles determines the destination of the lift and the point of origin for the subsequent lowering maneuver. The assumption is made that the operator loads the racks from two sides while facing the spindle being loaded. This keeps reach distances and lifting stresses to a minimum.

Lifting from the stockpile of rims does not require a significant reach. At the origin of the lift H has a nominal value. However, the horizontal reach increases at the destination when rims are placed on to spindles. For the calculation of the lifting limits, therefore, the greater horizontal displacement factor is used.

To the Lower Heat Treating Rack from the Stockpile

H is determined by the reach at the destination point
= 12″ (reach) + 6″ (body interference)
= 18″ (45 cm), as in task 1

V_{avg} = midpoint of the stockpile
= 2 × 8″ (rim depth), position of the grip
= 16″ (40 cm), as in task 2

D = destination − origin
= top of the lower rack − base of the rim
= 33″ (rack height) − 8″ (midpoint of stockpile measured at the base)
= 25″ (62.5 cm) travel

F = 252 rims/2 racks
= 126 rims/225 min.
= .5 lifts/min

yielding, discounting factors of

HF = .33   VF = .86   DF = .82   FF = .96

NIOSH Action Limit:

AL (lb) = 90(.33)(.86)(.82)(.96)
= 21.2 (9.1 kg)

To the Upper Heat Treating Rack from the Same Point of Origin

H,V,F as above

D = destination − origin
= 2 × 33″ (rack height) − 8″ (base of the rim at the origin)
= 58″ (145 cm) travel

yielding, discounting factors of

HF = .33 VF = .86 DF = .75 FF = .96

NIOSH Action Limit:

AL (lb) = 90(.33)(.86)(.75)(.96)
= 18.4 (8.4 kg)

Composite Average for this lift is determined by:

H, V as above

$\mathbf{D}_{avg}$ = average of the lower and upper racks
= 25″ + 58″/2 racks
= 41.5″ (104 cm)

$\mathbf{F}_{cum}$ = 252 lifts/225 min.
= 1.1 lifts/min.

yielding, discounting factors of

HF = .33 VF = .86 DF = .77 FF = .91

NIOSH Action Limit:

AL (lb) = 90(.33)(.86)(.77)(.91)
= 17.9 (8.1 kg)

The Action Limit for this task indicates that the lifting demands are excessive. Both racks are equally difficult to load. Snook and Ciriello do not have precise guidelines for this lift. By extrapolation, they would limit the task to less than 28 pounds (13 kg) for the composite lift. Current lifting demands exceed the guidelines.

Add to this the lowering component. Rims are lowered into place, three to a spindle. Taking the values of 17″ and 50″, respectively, (Table IV–I) for the average destinations produces limits of approximately 37 to

39 pounds (17 to 18 kg). These are the 90th percentile values for males obtained by interpolating from Snook and Ciriello. NIOSH does not have limits for lowering, although, to establish a guideline, the reciprocal lifting task might be assessed as was suggested earlier. Since the reciprocal lift is part of Task 4, the calculations appear there. Though some of the variables differ from the above, the calculated lifting limits are, nevertheless, very similar.

The limit for carrying is similar to the limit for lowering, both of which are less critical than the lifting component. Therefore, the limit for this task is established by the lift using the combined frequencies of lifting, lowering and carrying.

Composite limit for this task is determined by:

H_{avg}, V_{avg} and D_{avg} as above

$F_{cum} = 3 \times 1.1$ lifts/min

yielding, discounting factors of

| HF = .33 | VF = .86 | DF = .77 | FF = .73 |

NIOSH Action Limit

AL (lb) $= 90(.33)(.86)(.77)(.73)$
$= 14.3$ (6.5 kg)

Modifying Task 3 appears to be as important to controlling hazard potential as modifying Task 1. The horizontal displacement of the load during handling imposes major restrictions on the lifting.

Task 4—Unloading Heat Treating Racks and Loading Shipping Bins

Rims are taken from the heat treating racks and loaded into bins for shipping. This is the reverse of Task 3, during which rims are placed on to spindles in preparation for heat treating. Lifting, carrying and lowering characterize the manual handling activities of this task. The point of origin and the point of destination vary as in the preceding task. Rims are lifted off the spindles from one of three positions; the top, middle or base of the spindle and placed into one of layers in the shipping bins. For simplification an estimate is made of the average lift by calculating the lifting limits for removal of a rim from the intermediate position on the upper and lower racks respectively. The top rack is unloaded first; then work progresses to the bottom rack. The H factor is similar to that given before.

Upper Rack

H = as before
  = 18″ (45 cm)

V_{avg} = 33″ (lower rack) + 25″ (intermediate rim of the upper rack)
  = 58″ (145 cm) position of the grip

D_{avg} = destination − origin
  = spindle clearance (upper rack) − base of the intermediate rim
  = 2 × 33″ (rack height) − 50″ (base of second rim 8″ below the grip)
  = 16″ (40 cm) travel

F = 1 lift /2 min, as in preceding task

yielding, discounting factors of

HF = .33   VF = .72   DF = .89   FF = .96

NIOSH Action Limit:

AL (lb)   = 90(.33)(.72)(.89)(.96)
       = 18.3 (8.3 kg)

Lower Rack

H = 18″ (45 cm), as shown above

V_{avg} = bottom rack, intermediate rim
  = 25″ (62 cm) position of the grip

D_{avg} = destination − origin
  = spindle clearance (bottom rack) − base of the intermediate rim
  = 33″ (rack height) − 17″ (base of intermediate rim 8″ below grip)
  = 16″ (40 cm) travel

F = as above

yielding, discounting factors of

HF = .33   VF = .95   DF = .89   FF = .96

NIOSH Action Limit:

AL (lb)   = 90(.33)(.95)(.89)(.96)
       = 24 (11 kg)

Composite Average for this lift is determined by:

$H = 18''$ (45 cm), same

$V_{avg} = 25'' + 58''/2$ racks
     $= 41.5''$ (104 cm)

$D = 16''$ (40 cm), same for both racks

$F = 252$ rims/225 min $= 1.1$ lifts/min

yielding, discounting factors of

HF = .33   VF = .89   DF = .89   FF = .91

NIOSH Action Limit:

AL (lb) $= 90(.33)(.89)(.89)(.91)$
          $= 21.4$ (9.7 kg)

The lifting component exceeds guidelines. For other comments see the discussion about Task 3.

The lowering maneuver commences where the lifting maneuver terminates, at the top of the spindles. Using the intermediate rim as the average destination the following approach is taken. From the previous examples, the limit is determined for the countervailing lift which is amenable to calculation, whereas the lowering activity is not.

From Bin to Upper Rack

$H = 18''$ (45 cm), as before

$V = 20''$ (30 cm), as in task 1

D = destination − origin
   $= 2 \times 33''$ (upper rack height) $+ 8''$ (rim depth) $- 20''$ (avg position in bin)
   $= 54''$ (130 cm) travel distance

$F = .5$ lifts/min, as before

yielding, discounting factors of

HF = .33   VF = .9   DF = .76   FF = .96

NIOSH Action Limit

AL (lb) $= 90(.33)(.9)(.76)(.96)$
          $= 19.5$ (8.9 kg)

From Bin to Lower Rack

> H = 18″ (45 cm), as above
>
> V = 20″ (30 cm), as above
>
> D = destination − origin
> = 33″ (lower rack height) + 8″ (rim depth) − 20″ (avg position in bin)
> = 21″ (53 cm) travel distance
>
> F = .5 lifts / min, as above

yielding, discounting factors of

HF = .33	VF = .9	DF = .84	FF = .96

NIOSH Action Limit

> AL (lb)   = 90(.33)(.9)(.84)(.96)
> = 21.5 (9.8 kg)

Composite Average for the countervailing lift is:

> H = 18″ (45 cm)
>
> V = 20″ (50 cm)
>
> D_{avg} = 21″ + 54″/2 racks
> = 37.5″ (94 cm) travel distance
>
> F_{cum} = 1.1 lifts/min

yielding, discounting factors of

HF = .33	VF = .9	DF = .78	FF = .91

NIOSH Action Limit

> AL (lb)   = 90(.33)(.9)(.78)(.91)
> = 19 (8.6 kg)

Snook and Ciriello give a value of approximately 30 lbs (14 kg) as the guideline for lowering rims and almost the same for the lifting task. The calculated NIOSH guidelines are slightly more rigorous. Taking into account the cumulative frequency of all three handling tasks would further reduce the limit to 15 pounds (6.9 kg).

Integration of Multiple Components: Tasks 1 to 4 inclusive

Combining the previous tasks to determine a global approximation is not likely to be too meaningful. The tasks are too complex; the number of assumptions and liberal interpretations are already too many. The problem areas have been clearly established and intervention shown as necessary. There are two other factors which influence the ability to perform work. These relate to the interactive effects of multiple components. They are mentioned, though they are not be dealt with here. Both concern physiologic limitations. Energy demands of the combined tasks may exceed physiologic and endurance limits, because of the dynamic and continuous nature of the work. Secondly, activities take place near the furnaces adding an element of heat stress, which may impose further limitations on the ability to perform manual work.

Further Comments

It is important to note a few of the fundamental differences between the NIOSH approach and the Snook and Ciriello tables. Aside from differences in the way the two were derived, there are some differences in the way they are used. Manual handling limits and guidelines are based on the different strength capacities of males and females. The NIOSH Action Limit defines a level which is thought to be acceptable to 99% of males and over 75% of females. With the Snook and Ciriello tables that decision is left to the user. In the preceding assessments the criterion used was the 90th percentile male. Generally, this would not be the case. When designing and evaluating a task a criterion might be selected that incorporates a larger percentage of the industrial population, if, for example, females perform some of the manual handling. Using tables, and with a certain amount of interpolation, a range of lifting tasks can be assessed beyond those which are tabulated. The Snook and Ciriello tables are broad, in that tasks other than lifting can be assessed. A limitation arises when horizontal displacement during manual handling deviates from the tabulated data, a matter which is alluded to in the discussion of Task 2.

RECOMMENDATIONS

The above calculations and discussion have been presented to show the level of detail comprising the analysis of the tasks and to identify the tasks of greatest concern. In this case the job is the concern. There is simply too much manual handling required at almost every stage of the work. The following recommendations are presented in a stepwise progression in order of their complexity for implementation. Simple recommendations are usually preferred, because they have a greater likelihood of being implemented. They are more cost effective and less disruptive to work routines, and therefore more likely to be accepted. However, not all of the situations can be resolved in this manner and may require a combination of engineering and administrative controls.

There are a few simple steps that can be readily implemented to make the job easier for the furnace operator. Firstly, rims can be loaded directly onto heat treating racks after embossing. This alone would eliminate one unnecessary step, reducing manual handling by one-quarter. As it stands, stockpiling provides a buffer. However, there appears to be no reason why rims should be stacked on the floor rather than being directly placed onto spindle racks. There is no space limitation and there are plenty of empty racks available. Secondly, procedures might be changed. For example, it might be easier to load heat treating racks before stacking them. Furthermore, if both suggestions are implemented an additional benefit accrues, namely, that the current lift is converted into a lowering task. That is, rims would simply be lowered from the workbench on to the racks, instead of being lifted on to the top racks. Lowering is generally easier to perform than lifting.

Tote bins have one side which partially collapses to aid in loading and unloading. This currently serves no useful purpose, because the bins are unloaded and loaded from the floor. To reduce the physical work the tote bins could be placed on an elevated platform near the workbench with the side opened to facilitate unloading. In other words, if the bins are lifted, then the operator is spared some of the lifting. A variable height rather than fixed height platform would be better still, one that self-adjusts according to the load. There are scissor tables, spring-supported platforms, and operator-controlled types available. Their use would eliminate much of the heavy manual work associated with unloading and loading of the tote bins.

One other simple recommendation to consider would be to load rims on end, rather than lying flat. Two potential benefits might result from this. One, it could facilitate unloading: rims could easily be rolled out of the bins onto the bench instead of being lifted. Two, it is more efficient to pack the tote bins this way. The space requirements even for a 14″ rim, according to the present stacking arrangement of 2×3 rows $\times$ 3 layers, uses a minimum of 28″ $\times$ 42″ $\times$ 26″ (which includes 2″ for the cardboard/wood spacers). Within a 44″ $\times$ 54″ $\times$ 38″ bin this leaves plenty of unused space. There is enough room to accommodate twice as many rims. Standing on end there is enough room for 3×6 rows $\times$ 2 layers which would occupy a space of 42″ $\times$ 48″ $\times$ 29″ (including 1″ spacers). This improvement in efficiency, perhaps important for other reasons as well, for example, in shipping, translates into labor savings and reduces the number of totes manually handled. Implementing these recommendations will not materially change the job in any other way, save for reducing the physical demands.

Loading and unloading of the heat treating racks is another area of high priority. As with all lifts examined, the biomechanical stresses are aggravated disproportionately by one factor, the H factor. With the tote bins the effect of H can be minimized by converting the task from lifting to pulling, sliding and/or rolling as described in the preceding paragraphs. To reduce the H factor, heat treating racks can be placed on an inclined platform as shown in Figure IV-12. If tilted to the near vertical position the operator can simply slide the rims off the spindles. The overhead hoist can also be used to manipulate the racks. Thus, by implementing relatively minor changes of procedure and layout, the job can be transformed into something less physically demanding.

The purpose of this job is to produce heat treated parts, but a large portion of the manual labor is indirectly related to a secondary function, labelling. The first two tasks are dedicated to this one activity. This begs the question of whether the process of stamping and identifying rims can be replaced with a much simpler system. Using an eleven-pound sledge to manually emboss 250 rims is just one added aggravation in a physically demanding job. Indeed, there are probably various alternatives including self-adhesive metallic labels, wire loops with tags, clips, etc. If labelling can be done while the rims are still on the heat treating racks then additional handling may be avoided, eliminating possibly one half of the manual handling.

If the method of tagging rims is of little consequence, then further options can be explored. For example, it was previously suggested that

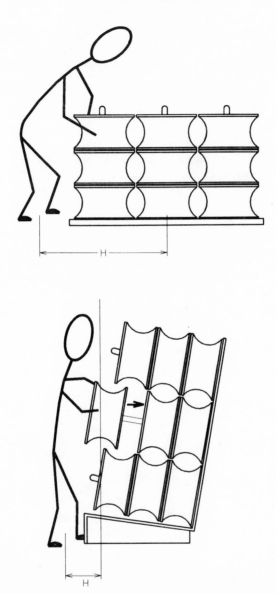

Figure IV-12. The loading and unloading of rims from the heat treating racks would be substantially improved if the H factor was reduced. See text for discussion.

rims be stacked on end, rather than lying flat. In this arrangement a rod can be pushed through the hubs to allow the hoist to do the unloading and loading. The existing heat treating racks could probably be modified by welding mounting brackets on to the spindles to hold the rods horizontally. The supplier would need to agree to ship the rims on end.

Rods might have to be provided. There is even a strong possibility that the supplier has interests which overlap. One might anticipate somewhat the same problems at the supplier's end. Obviously, the suppliers employees load the *greenware* and unload the finished stock.

Other more technically elaborate possibilities exist, although further details will not be given. These might include:

(1) heat treating racks with telescopic spindles
(2) tote bins and heat treating racks designed to marry
(3) tote bins with trays to facilitate mechanical loading and unloading.

Case V

THE RAILROADERS' ROSTER

As a trainmaster Mike is far removed from the day-to-day activities associated with railroading. At one time Mike was just one of the crew working the trains. From the junior position of signalman he worked his way to becoming a foreman, and later a locomotive engineer. From there he continued to move ahead, taking on a variety of new challenges and responsibilities. He was bright, motivated, and learned quickly. That is what eventually catapulted him into one of the top positions in the region. Now his days are occupied with far broader concerns about managing the railroading business in a region covering some 80,000 square miles and servicing eleven major cities.

One of these concerns derived from the Hillworth train disaster which had taken place in a bordering region and sent a jolt throughout the whole industry. A freight train and a passenger train collided head-on along a single stretch of transcontinental route. The accident investigators said that alcohol was implicated in the cause of the accident. This was no surprise to Mike, but he wondered whether it was the only problem or even the major one. He remembered signalmen, and probably a few engineers too, who had come to work "under the influence" back in the days when he was the foreman on the crew. That alcohol increases the risks of accident is indisputable. And, in fact, the company had instituted an employee assistance program six years ago to deal with such problems. But whether the engineer at Hillworth had missed a signal, was too slow to react because of the alcohol, or had fallen asleep because of the alcohol, wasn't the only issue, thought Mike. He well knew that falling asleep was always a possibility, even without the alcohol.

Minor accidents, he said to himself, are always happening, or at least minor in comparison to Hillworth. More often than not, nobody was hurt, he thought. Invariably with large equipment like railcars, locomotives and freight, however, even the minor accidents were costly. And even if freight and equipment escaped damage there was still the loss of productive time spent in getting the railcars back on the track, as well as the costs of employing a track repair crew, a crane, and so on.

The thought of an accident waiting to happen did not sit well with Mike, not that he had any basis for his apprehension. On the contrary he often cynically expressed the view that accidents were a cost of doing business. As far as he was able to ascertain, human error was usually the cause and there wasn't much that could be done about that, short of replacing people with machines and, as he put it, getting rid of a few of the "less capable" workers.

Mike knew of other unresolved problems with the train crews, although he could not quite pin down the cause-and-effect relationships. Certainly, attitude in general, whether of management or workers, was a concern. Always, there was a sense of friction between those working inside and the train crews working outside. Service and commitment to work, these were other things that bothered him. Mike knew these problems would not be resolved quickly, if at all, nor did he expect them to be. But he knew things were somehow wrong, and these didn't derive from the inadequacies of the employees. Perhaps it was the anxiety that accompanied his position of responsibility, perhaps it was just Mike, and maybe it was because deep down he was still one of the boys despite the gap between them, but he had a feeling that something else was going to happen. He was not sure that he could verbalize it, but the thought of an accident in the waiting was unsettling.

As he thought more about it, Mike began to remember how easy it was to fall asleep at the controls. He even recalled cursing the locomotive engineer for failing to heed signals when he was foreman. But, he was not too quick to criticize. He remembered when he became an engineer that it was difficult to stay awake through the monotonous night, or even by day, and to stay alert at all times while operating an engine. It seemed almost to be part of the job.

Perhaps the workload was just too much, he thought. When things were busy, or the shop was short of engineers, overtime was plentiful. Shortages often happened, and still do, he mused, especially during the summer and Christmas seasons with some engineers away on holidays, and others simply booking off for whatever personal reasons. Working two shifts back-to-back during such times was not unusual. One double shift was not so bad, thought Mike, but if more overtime arrived later in the week it was difficult to say no. The pay was too good to pass up and the money always was spoken for.

Management had at least made some attempt to increase the local pool of locomotive engineers to overcome these shortages, but admittedly, not much had changed in the rail yards over the years. The large cities in the region have attractions, but the smaller centers are dead-end places for railroaders. Workers are generally less willing to work the spare boards in these small godforsaken places. At the end of a road trip or a shift there isn't much to do in one of these often remote places. Having a drink at the end of the work stint offers one, and for some, the only simple pleasure available. If crews are destined to be working in one of the small centers, then working "the road" travelling between cities and towns, rather than working shifts in the small rail yards, is more highly preferred. The pay is better and the monthly mileage quota can be achieved in two weeks of steady work by putting in long hours. Sometimes the road crews, anxious to get in their quotas, work twenty-four to forty-eight hours with little or no rest, earning a longer time off or positioning themselves for overtime if the opportunity presents itself.

Maybe, surmised Mike, while alcohol certainly contributed to the problems, perhaps excessive working hours and even sheer boredom also required some consideration. The dilemma was what to do about these problems.

The regular workweek in the rail yard is forty hours, consisting of five eight-hour shifts. The shifts are assigned on the basis of seniority using a bidding process. The best shifts go to railroaders with the most seniority. The bidding takes place twice per year, in the spring and in the fall. Yard crews may bid for a position on the road, and vice versa, road crews may elect to work in the yard. Those who lack the seniority to hold a regular shift in the yard, or a regular run on the road, work the *spare board*, filling in as needed when vacancies occur. Yard and road work each have their separate spare boards.

Work is assigned by a yard master to each train crew at the beginning of the shift or road trip. The work outlines where the crew will be required and the type of duties to be performed there. Experienced foremen and enginemen are quick to evaluate the level of effort and amount of time to be spent in accomplishing their assigned objectives and to determine their pace of work. The pace of work is not only governed by the amount of work but also by the experience of the crew, their motivation, their respect for the yard master and other factors. Occasionally the yard master will receive an unexpected call requesting the railroad to provide a rush service, which in turn is passed along to the crew to be added to their existing list of routine duties. For example, an industrial client might need one of the freight cars to be switched to another unloading bay.

Overtime is paid for shifts extending beyond eight hours and for work performed on statutory holidays. The overtime rate is time plus a half. This rate is paid on the entire overtime activity when the shift is extended by more than one hour. When the overtime period is less than one hour, only the regular hourly rate is paid on the overtime portion. Overtime rates are not owed to those who work extra shifts beyond their weekly duties, nor are the workers obliged to accept the work. Vacant positions are filled from the "spare board" first, then in a revolving order based on seniority. There are no other constraints preventing a worker from accepting an extra shift other than availability and fitness for work. Locomotive engineers and signalmen are, therefore, free to go from one shift to the next without a pause if they are called upon to do so. The process is self-regulated in this regard.

The current system, in fact, rewards and promotes extended overtime. Each crew determines the pace of work, while the amount of work is determined by demand for service and the number of crews performing the labor. This allows each crew certain liberties in determining the pace of work and in striving for longer overtime. The expression in the industry is slow wheelin', meaning to take a long time to perform a maneuver.

ASSIGNMENT

Imagine you've been invited by the major railroad company that Mike works for to consider this whole problem of work shifts and duration of work, with particular reference to railroading. Talking with Mike has revealed a lot of anecdotal evidence like the foregoing, but you want some more hard facts to corroborate your investigation.

Wanting to trace the issue further, you ask to see a record typical of the hours worked by an engineman in the yard. While Mike is arranging with the shop steward for a copy of an engineman's log he comments, "If you think there is some kind of a problem in the yard, then it is probably worse on the road". You obtain a logbook eventually. From the conversation with Mike and the logbook you are able to extract the following additional information.

The log book you have borrowed belongs to Len who is an engineman with twenty-one years of service, most of it spent in the relatively small rail yard where he currently works. You recognize that his log book may not be representative of other more senior enginemen. Nor does his log book reveal any telling information about work on the road.

His log shows that he held a regular shift for most of the summer holiday season, albeit one of the less desirable shifts. During the past month, illustrated in Table V–I, he held the swing shift. The swing shift, as the name might imply, works eight hours on Thursday and Friday afternoons beginning at 3:00 P.M., followed by eight hours on Saturday and Sunday mornings at 7:00 A.M., then again at midnight Sunday evening. Monday through Wednesday are days off. The swing shift provides coverage and client service when other shifts are idle at the end of their workweek; consequently, it is different from the other shifts which work straight mornings, afternoons or evenings.

Table V-I
LEN'S OVERTIME (OT) DURING 4-WEEK PERIOD

	Work Week			
	Week 1	Week 2	Week 3	Week 4
Day				
Thursday	no OT	80 min	no OT	6:30*
Friday	130 min	no OT	95 min	110 min
Saturday	no OT	165 min	no OT	75 min
Sunday (am)	no OT	15 min	105 min	no OT
Sunday (pm)	no OT	no OT	65 min	no OT
Monday	7:00*	day off	day off	day off
Tuesday	day off	day off	22:00*	day off
Wednesday	day off	24:00	day off	day off

*Extra shift at regular wages. Time indicates when shift began.

Len's paychecks must have been very good this past month with the overtime and extra shifts. The first week was long, because of the extra shift Monday morning on his day off. This seemed to set the pattern for the entire month. The following weeks were equally busy as indicated by the record of his overtime. Note that only once during the month was the overtime period less than one hour in duration.

The assignment is simple, although it will require some consideration. Discuss Len's work schedule. Do you find anything in it to be concerned about? If so, what advice will you offer Mike when you make your report, with respect to Len in particular and work schedules in general?

THE RAILROADERS' ROSTER SOLUTION

Before examining the specifics of this case consider some general comments on such matters as alertness, monotony, duration of work, sleep, circadian rhythms, and shift work. All of these will help Mike understand the problems you see and how they interact.

Apart from the skills required, the ability to perform continued tracking or monitoring at a high level, a task which comprises most of an engineman's work, is largely determined by the presence or absence of the phenomenon termed arousal. Arousal is the name given to the condition of physical and mental alertness which characterizes the awake and active state. It is under the control of a special neural network, the reticular activating system (RAS). The RAS network is stimulated by the senses, what you see, what you hear, etc., and by messages from the brain. For whatever reason, whether a self-generated thought, or information from the senses, the brain instructs itself and the rest of the body to remain alert, or to increase the level of alertness already existing. Where no such stimulus arises, perhaps in the absence of adequate stimuli, or in boredom, or under monotonous conditions, and where the stimuli are not adequately conveyed as is the case with alcohol consumption and certain drugs, the alertness gradually diminishes, leading in some cases to sleep. That this fact occurs amongst trainmen has been documented in Japan and Germany (Fraser, 1989).

While sleep, of course, may occur from diminished arousal, the need for sleep derives from the body's requirements for restoration, which are both natural and the result of fatigue. Naturally occurring sleepiness is influenced by the existence of intrinsically defined, regularly occurring diurnal body rhythms, known as circadian rhythms (circadian means "round about a day"). Human physiology, and to a more intangible extent, human psychology, have evolved to respond to the regular sequence of light and dark that make up the twenty-four-hour day, such that for example the natural tendency is to be awake by day and asleep at night. Probably all physiological and psychological functions are affected to a greater or lesser extent, some more obvious or more readily measurable than others. Thus, the volume and content of various bodily fluids and secretions changes during the night, particularly while sleeping, while measurable functions such as heart rate, body temperature, blood pressure and so on tend to be reduced. Behavior, in the psychological sense, is also affected. Sleep demand and sleep capacity are greatest during the night hours, while alertness and mental capacity are reduced.

Circadian rhythms, therefore, can be grossly disturbed by shift work. One of the major problems is that shift work requires the worker to perform at a high level during a period when, at least initially, the individual is not prepared for it and the body is in a state of transition trying to adapt to the new circumstances. Should alertness and physical abilities be compromised further by lack of sleep from excessive overtime in preceding days or weeks, the problem will be all the more aggravated.

It is possible to modify the inherent rhythm and pattern, but not with ease. Some degree of adaptation can occur within about 6–10 days of continued reinforcement, but it takes weeks, if not months to effect a complete change. The change is easier if accompanied by a change in exposure to light and dark, as for example in changing six or eight time zones. Gradual as opposed to abrupt changes can also ease the transition. Repeated change over a short period of time, as in relatively frequent shift changes, does not allow adaptation to occur and may additionally disrupt social forces which help to maintain the rhythms.

The appropriateness of overtime and the duration of working hours have been studied since World War I. The accumulated experience, backed up by controlled experiments, have demonstrated that in normal circumstances the optimum work routine is found within an 8-hour day and a 40–50-hour workweek. This routine is not always feasible, but where working hours are extended to, say, 12 hours, each three to four days of work should be followed by three to four free days. Workers can indeed maintain a 16-hour day for weeks at a stretch, with appropriate motivation or reward, but inevitably such exposure leads to reduced proficiency, chronic fatigue, reduced safety and eventually ill-health.

Keep these thoughts in mind as we now return to the case at hand. There are three separate yet related issues that might draw your attention. One is the spillover effect on the regular work schedule resulting from extra shiftwork. The spillover is due to disturbance of the body's circadian rhythms. Similar physiological and psychological demands are imposed by the variable shift routine entrenched within the swing shift. The second consideration is whether there is adequate opportunity for rest when overtime arrives. Overtime disrupts the regular work-rest cycle, shortening the rest period, and at times compounding the disruptive effect on the circadian pattern. The third factor is the generally permissive nature of the system which does not define restrictions on extra duties.

Schedules should be shifted gradually to allow body rhythms time to adjust. Taking on an extra shift or working straight through without rest, as is done on the road, suddenly jars the rhythms out of their natural synchronicity when sleep is compromised. Once disturbed, the rhythms take nearly two weeks to fully recover, hence the need for a graduated adjustment. Clearly, anyone working the swing shift does not have the opportunity to maintain their physiological cycles in balance.

As noted, alertness is one of the mental functions that follow a diurnal pattern. When a person is disoriented from their normal sleep routine, sleepiness results and judgment may be affected, either of which may contribute to accidents. Maintaining a routine sleep schedule is critical, although the time of day for sleeping is less important, provided conditions are appropriate. The regular sleep does not need to occur at night to maintain the body rhythms, but must occur at a regular time during the twenty-four-hour cycle.

Len's log shows that he averaged about eleven and a half hours of overtime per week during the month. The amount of overtime is not the real concern. Work can be sustained at these levels for weeks, if not more, as has already been noted. The problem is the shorter time available for rest away from work. Estimated conservatively, suppose it takes Len half an hour each way to and from work, effectively reducing the off time available for resting by one hour per day. His Friday shift during the first week earned him two hours and ten minutes of overtime. He returned to work the following morning at seven o'clock. The maximum time for his rest was therefore only four hours and fifty minutes, cut short by the overtime of the previous evening and the travel to and from work. If by chance he compromised a sleep period, especially following closely upon a previous loss of sleep due to working an extra shift, then re-adjustment of physiologic rhythms would be still further aggravated.

On the basis of the foregoing, then, you can advise Mike that, because of the nature of the work schedules, disruptions to normal physiologic rhythms are inevitable amongst the engineers and are likely to impact on their alertness. The swing shift is a conspicuous example of a schedule that can be very disruptive. Indeed, from the perspective of maintaining a balanced physiological burden, you consider that the current practices may be contributing to the causes of accidents. While you recognize that hiring or training additional crews would be expensive, you point out that the costs could well be offset by reduction in the hidden costs of lost productive time and damages from injury and accidents. Although the facts are not available here, it would be instructive to determine the relationship between accidental events and the work schedules of the crew.

Case VI

THE FRUSTRATED FIREFIGHTER

A small municipality, population about 240,000, has been hiring men to fill vacancies in the fire brigade. A very fit 25-year-old female has applied for a second time. Two years ago, during the previous hiring session, she was turned down. Admittedly, she missed the acceptance grade on the pre-screening test, as did a number of other candidates, all of whom were male, but she missed it only by a fraction. She is still eager to join the ranks, however; the pay is good, the challenge exciting, and for her the inherent rewards far exceed the remuneration.

Being very persistent, strong-willed, and knowing what to expect, she undergoes physical training before the test session, vowing to gain a place on the roster. This time she successfully meets all of the physical challenge test criteria. Now the municipality really has no choice but to hire her, although she is the only female firefighter on staff. In fact, during recent times there is no recollection of females even applying for the position.

The municipality, being very sensitive to the human rights codes, recognizes the threshold it has just crossed by inviting a female to join in what has traditionally been sacred male ground and, while accepting the inevitable in this instance, realizes that some further investigation of the pre-employment selection process is in order to determine whether the test criteria are now or could have been considered unfairly exclusionary in the past, particularly with respect to women. Information resulting from such a review could be used by Personnel to shape future policy and hiring practices, not just within the Fire Department, but, at least in principle, within the entire municipal framework.

BACKGROUND INFORMATION

Firefighting

Fire-fighting tasks and associated activities can at times be among the most strenuous and physically demanding of any occupation. Climbing a steep ladder while carrying a formidable load even for short durations of less than 15 minutes, or fire fighting for periods of 1–2 hours can, depending on the circumstances, require more energy than chopping wood, sawing logs, stacking concrete blocks, or lifting heavy boxes. Whole-body work in fire fighting may require more than 10 kcal/min, while the upper body alone may require in excess of 7 kcal/min. These levels of energy expenditure require extremely heavy effort. Only about 30 percent of a male work force would be able to sustain such activity for longer than 15–20 minutes. At these levels even fewer persons have the necessary aerobic capacity to continue for a full hour without taking a break.

Physical Fitness Testing

In the municipality under consideration candidates being considered for the position of firefighter are required to perform some or all of the following physical fitness tests. Before the tests are administered, the candidate must present a copy of a declaration signed by a physician stating that there is no medical objection to his/her participation in the testing. The tests include the following.

The candidate must be able to:

(1) run 1½ miles within 12 minutes;

(2) perform 25 bent-knee sit-ups within 90 seconds;

(3) complete 5 consecutive chin-ups from a starting position with the arms completely extended and the palms pronated;

(4) perform 10 uninterrupted push-ups in the horizontal position;

(5) lift a 125 lb barbell from the floor and carry it for a distance of 100 ft without stopping;

(6) manipulate a weight from the standing and squatting positions while performing a calisthenic maneuver as prescribed in the following manner:

Beginning with the feet set apart to shoulder width, with the body standing erect, and a 15 lb weight placed midway between the two feet:

- bend over, pick up the weight with both hands, lift it to waist height;
- without letting go of the grip, by squatting down, touch the weight to the floor on the left side at a distance not closer than 12 inches from the left foot;
- stand up, raise the weight to waist level and proceed to do the same for the right side of the body;
- perform a series of 7 moves for each side, the total of the 14 exercises to be completed within 35 seconds.

(7) walk the entire length of a 20 ft beam (width, 4 in) carrying a segment of fire hose weighing at least 20 lbs without stepping off the beam;

(8) climb a 35 ft ladder on to the training tower;

(9) drag a water-filled $2\frac{1}{2}$ in hose and nozzle a distance of at least 90 feet;

(10) unravel a section of hose by pulling the nozzle up to the window sill of the training tower. The hose must touch the window sill and must be lowered to the ground hand over hand, as if being fed. This is to be repeated sequentially for a total of 4 times. Warning is given to the candidate that this is a strenuous task, requiring the subject to pace his/her activities. Performance is graded.

ASSIGNMENT

You have been given a description of the pre-employment fitness testing protocol used by the Fire Department. Acting as an ergonomic consultant, prepare a report, as if to the City Council, outlining your views as to whether the tests are likely to be valid assessments of the physical demands. Bear in mind that the job of fire fighting is known to be extremely demanding. It may well be that the concept underlying these tests might be considered a reflection of the simple realities inherent in the job, not restrictive of females per se, but of all persons lacking certain strength, abilities and capacities. In other words, while the criteria may be so stringent that most females and many males would be excluded, they may not necessarily be considered discriminative against women. Your conclusions may side one way or the other.

Another way of viewing or rephrasing the issue is to speculate on the following. Suppose the female candidate failed again on the second round, and, being disillusioned with the process, she brings the issue before a human rights tribunal. Would the testing protocol be ruled valid?

The question relates to what is called content validity, or in other words having a direct bearing on the demands of the job. For a test to be content valid it must fulfill the following criteria:

(a) the knowledge, skills, and abilities being tested must be critical and not peripherally related to successful job performance;

(b) the tests should accurately reflect the relative importance of the attributes on the job and for which the tests are applied; and

(c) the level of difficulty of the test material should match the level of difficulty of the job.

THE FRUSTRATED FIREFIGHTER SOLUTION*

This scenario discusses the potentially contentious situation of dis-criminatory hiring practices. While perhaps initiated by an apparent controversy over gender discrimination, the real question is not whether females are being discriminated against, but whether the pre-employment screening tests are in fact fair and valid. Tests are valid in law only if they are predictors of ability to perform the essential duties of a job. Hence, there are two criteria for screening tests which need to be met. One, screening tests must be predictors of ability to perform fire-fighting duties; and, two, the tests must relate to the essential attributes of the job.

Tests 7–10 inclusive appear to assess certain physical capacities funda-mental to the job. Let us accept for the moment that they do. The same cannot be said for the first six tests. It is in no way obvious that a person's ability to do push-ups or sit-ups will be a direct measure of his/her ability to perform fire-fighting duties. Indeed, while exercise tests in general may be somewhat indicative of overall strength, endurance, fitness and cardiovascular tone, all of which are necessary qualities in a candidate, they have nothing to do with the actual duties required on the job.

The relevance of the test(s) in relation to the job is important. Some candidates may be capable of performing the job and yet fail to pass certain tests. Likewise, a proportion of viable candidates passing all of the tests may be incapable of doing the job. Tests which closely emulate the actual tasks are more likely to avoid these concerns and to have credibility. They are also likely to circumvent any of the biases that arise because of differences between male and female strength and other physiologic capacities. In a related matter, if certain criteria can be satisfied through basic training, then the objective of screening is to

*For additional information, refer to Misner, J.E., Boileau, R.A. and Plowman, S.A., Development of placement tests for firefighting. *Appl. Ergo.,* V20, 218–224, 1989.

identify those who can be trained with the least investment of energy and resources.

If challenged legally it would be difficult to sustain an argument that certain exercise/fitness criteria are a pre-requisite for hiring, a must to getting the job done, when undoubtedly a group of incumbents on-the-job do not meet these very same criteria. Yet they function adequately. How? Because they can do the essential demands of the job. Thus, testing must relate to the essential demands of the job and must be able to predict functional capacity to meet those demands. Test 5, for example, seeks to determine strength and the ability of the firefighter to move a non-ambulatory or injured person from a place of risk to a place of relative safety. From this perspective the test may be seen to have some value, but the content must also have a direct bearing on the task demands. Would failure to lift and carry a barbell weighing 125 lbs preclude a would-be firefighter from safely evacuating an adult from danger? Not necessarily, given the freedom to choose a lifting strategy. The injured party could be carried out piggyback, slouched over the shoulder in the classic "firefighter's lift", or using some other method. If the purpose of the weight lifting test is to predict whether a candidate is able to evacuate a person of given size, then the test should be set up to examine this.

Does the balance beam test relate to an essential demand? If a physical demands analysis were performed, could this test be substantiated? Agility is a highly desirable quality in a prospective candidate, but does it play a meaningful part in the day-to-day tasks of the firefighter? What are the day to day tasks of a firefighter? Shouldn't a physical demands analysis of their duties be consulted or even conducted before any tests are devised? Fire fighters do more than just fight fires. They are part of the first line emergency response team called upon for resuscitation, freeing trapped passengers caught in twisted wreckage, controlling chemical spills, and so on. How do these duties factor into the testing protocol?

The relative merits of one test versus the next might be discussed at length. The validity of some of the tests is clearly questionable, although obviously some might be suitable. Even these, however, would need to be verified. Owing to the different level of effort and fatigue associated with each test, it would be imperative not only to establish a standard test battery but also to follow a fixed sequence ensuring fairness to all candidates.

Case VII

THE LITIGIOUS LAB TECH

A large manufacturing company which produces agricultural chemicals maintains a quality control department with a sophisticated chemical laboratory for product testing. The company has been in business for many years and is generally well regarded by the employees and the small town community in which this production facility resides. Recently, a situation has developed in the laboratory which has left the technicians in the laboratory, the supervisor and the personnel department with mixed feelings about a coworker.

A laboratory technician seeking compensation for an elbow injury has made a claim to the Workers' Compensation Board. The company has just been notified that the claim has been approved and payment is about to be processed. The company is disputing the claim, arguing that the work of the lab tech was not the cause of her injury. Should the claim be substantiated the company will suffer financial loss and its rating with the compensation board will be impaired, affecting the status of future claims.

The employee in question is a 43-year-old female of fifteen years standing with the company. She is employed as a chemical laboratory technician in the quality control department. She seems to enjoy her work and over the years has developed close friendships among fellow staff. However, in recent months, since her return from a vacation, she reported having pain while performing routine elements of her work and has seen various physicians about the problem. When the problem did not seem to resolve itself and therapy proved unsuccessful, she filed for compensation. Here is what the records show.

THE EMPLOYEE

Name: Janice S.   Marital status: married
Height: 5'6"   3 children: ages 9, 8, 5
Weight: 134 lbs
Age: 43

Education: High school diploma, 6 month Technical College Certificate
Employment History: Prior employment in clerical positions
Current Position: Senior laboratory technician
Hobbies and Recreation: Baking, knitting and crochet, leisurely strolls

THE WORK

There are six other technicians in quality control besides Janice, all of them female, with one female supervisor. The technician's job comprises the performance of several routine tests, each of which involves standard bench chemistry. None of the tests is complicated in terms of the wet chemistry involved. Some of the tests are simple instrument measurements which take no more than a minute or so to perform. Other tests follow a step-by-step cookbook approach, lasting up to seventy-five minutes. In all, approximately twelve to fifteen different tests may be routinely performed on any given chemical product. While the specific measurements and tests vary from product to product, many are the same.

The following laboratory procedures are among those most often performed by technicians in quality control to test the purity of samples:

1. *Melting point:* This is determined for every batch of product manufactured in the plant. A capillary-sized tube is packed with sample using a tiny plunger and is then set into an oil bath. The bath is heated and when melting begins the temperature is read. The task is done seated. The majority of the time is spent simply waiting for the transformation to occur. Only in the final moments is close vigilance required. The test requires fifteen to twenty minutes to perform.

2. *Titration procedures:* These are based on well-known chemical reactions which induce a color change in one solution by the addition of another. The exact point of color change is measured using a graduated glass column, or burette, which is filled from the top and allowed to evacuate out of the other end. The rate of titration is controlled by governing the flow of solution out of the burette. As the endpoint approaches, close vigilance is required to avoid overshooting. Usually it is more convenient for the technician to stand rather than sit when observing and performing the titration, and to bend forward as needed. The titration itself takes little time, perhaps fifteen minutes in total, but

the preparation, which may include distillation, extraction, and/or other chemical procedures beforehand, may take up to an hour.

3. *Gravimetric analysis:* A simple weight determination using a sensitive electronic balance is performed in conjunction with other procedures that measure the ash content or moisture and volatile components of a specimen. The task of weighing is performed in well under five minutes, while the technician remains seated in front of the balance. The other preparation procedures occupy the majority of the time, namely, twenty-five to fifty minutes.

4. *Colorimetry:* The color of a specimen is subjectively graded against calibration standards.

5. *Viscosity:* This is read from a hydrometer which is floated in the fluid specimen.

6. *Acidity/alkalinity:* An electronic probe is inserted into the specimen and displays the acidity or alkalinity in terms of pH. No preparation is required.

7. *Percent solids:* A pre-weighed quantity of specimen is washed through a sintered glass funnel using a solvent. Once dried, the specimen is re-weighed to measure the change in weight.

8. *Gas chromatography/high pressure liquid chromatography:* On a regular basis the technicians spend one week per rotation working with gas chromatography or high pressure liquid chromatography. The chromatography devices are complex and sophisticated electronic instruments. Sample preparation and instrument adjustment can take up to three hours depending upon the type of samples previously analyzed by the instrument of choice. Once the analysis begins, however, the process is fully automatic and runs alone without the need for constant feedback. A warning is given in case of an instrument failure, but from time to time the operator also checks to ensure that all is running smoothly and that the desired output is being generated.

Approximately 20% of the time is spent in cleanup, disassembling glassware, returning equipment to its place of storage, filling the dishwasher, rinsing glassware, and so on.

WORK DEMANDS AND ENVIRONMENT

The technicians in the quality control department rotate from job to job gaining personal experience in all facets of the laboratory work. All of the technicians have similar jobs in terms of the physical, intellectual, and skill requirements of the job and their duties. The company and the employees are both satisfied with this arrangement. Also, during employee absences work can continue uninterrupted.

Bench chemistry, as many of you are aware of, or even have experienced, entails a lot of standing while hovering over a bench, pouring one solution into a vessel or extracting another, peering into glassware, titrating drop by drop to obtain a color change, evaporating a liquid, or any of a number of other activities. Many of these tasks involve awkward upper body positions, postures, and motions, the maintenance of which can require considerable static work. At times the head and eyes are fixed in one position, with one arm, elbow, and shoulder splayed in another direction while the hands move about the profusion of glassware reaching ever so carefully to apply a clamp, adjust a knob or dial, and so on. The head may be perched atop a stiff neck while the hands decant a minute amount of liquid, weigh out micro quantities of a substance, or record results in a notebook. Many of these are precision activities fraught with concentration and muscle tension, although little in the way of manual work is required. They are activities that are generalized, however, and don't tend to be localized to one or two joint systems.

Strength requirements, in fact, are minimal. Occasionally heavy gas cylinders need to be replaced, but these are maneuvered by rolling, and transported by cart, commonly by maintenance workers and rarely by the technicians. Extended reaches are sometimes required when setting up glassware, initiating a titration, and so on, but these are relatively infrequent and do not involve significant amounts of static work. There may be brief periods of postural discomfort from standing in one spot for too long or from stooping forward to observe something. However, stepladders and stools are accessible and are used when work permits.

The technicians are competent and know their duties. Accuracy and prudence are stressed. Laboratory staff are kept busy, but not overburdened. They have some autonomy and freedom in planning their workday. From experience they know which tests to perform. They work five days per week with weekends off. They have good vacations and benefits.

By most standards the working environment is relatively comfortable. Although this laboratory facility is older, the room is temperature-controlled and has a view and a certain amount of natural lighting. All of the essential safety features are provided, and indeed the lab has a good safety record with no major injuries.

CHRONOLOGY OF THE CASE

Just prior to reporting her complaint the employee in question, Janice S., was off work for a three-week vacation during which she assisted her husband in renovating her house. Shortly after returning to work she reported difficulty in performing some of her normal duties without experiencing pain. She claimed that elevated, extended, or reaching motions of her upper arms and shoulders caused pain, chiefly in her right elbow. The pain subsided considerably when her arms were motionless. Although it persisted, she managed to hold out for the duration of the first week.

The pain continued into the second week, forcing the employee to call and advise her employer that she would not be attending work. During the next three days she was absent from work, but continued to keep the employer informed. On the third day, with no relief from pain, she consulted her personal physician who provided her with a note for her employer. The note advised that she should remain off work for an additional two weeks, if not longer. She was also given treatment to counter inflammation and pain and told to refrain from activity for the next few weeks, which she did.

She returned to work two and a half weeks after seeing her physician and was assigned "modified" duties in the form of clerical work. Then she returned to her usual job for a few days before again complaining of elbow discomfort. She has been off work ever since.

ABSENTEEISM RECORD

The absenteeism record of Janice has been quite unremarkable until recently. Work absences have been limited in number and always appear to be the result of activities unrelated to the job. Unfortunately, the cause of these absences is recorded quite vaguely, and, of course, access to her medical records is not available. In addition to any medical factors, there may have been undetermined personal, family, or other factors involved. Previous absences may or may not relate to the present injury, but this cannot be judged. The record merely indicates the explanation given by the employee to her supervisor. The records show absences on the following days for the following reasons:

Date	Reason Given
January 26, 1988	sore throat
November 28, 1988	"flu"
January 19, 1989	cold in the head
May 31, 1989	stomach ache
June 9, 1989	undefined illness
June 21–23, 1989	chest cold
October 4, 1989	undefined illness
January 2–February 9, 1990	gynecological surgery
June 25–July 13, 1990	Tennis elbow
August 1, 1990 onwards	Tennis elbow
February 11, 1991	Compensation awarded

RESUME OF THE MEDICAL HISTORY

As has already been noted, after three weeks vacation Janice S. returned to work on June 18, 1990, but almost immediately complained of discomfort in her right elbow. When she visited her personal physician one and a half weeks later (June 27, 1990) some swelling was visible and the condition was described to her as tennis elbow, known by its medical name as epicondylitis. She was treated with analgesics and anti-inflammatory drugs and told to refrain from using the elbow. She stayed off work for the remainder of the week and for an additional two weeks. She then returned to work wearing a pad splint and was given light duties for a couple of weeks before resuming her old job. Within a few days, however, she was off work again for the same problem and did not return from that point forward. It is not known what she did after leaving her work.

Upon the advice of her physician Janice began physiotherapy sessions in late August. During the first week she received different treatments including ultrasound and whirlpool baths. She reported to her physician that each treatment seemed to make matters worse. The physician asked her to be patient (no pun intended!) and to continue with the treatments for a short while more. After two further weeks of physiotherapy the treatments were discontinued. She was told to rest her arm and that with time the elbow would heal.

In early November, Janice was seen by an orthopedic surgeon who confirmed the diagnosis and supported the view of her personal physician that she had become permanently disabled and was unable to return to her job. Later that month Janice also visited a specialist in occupational medicine. He was in disagreement with the other two doctors and of the opinion that Janice was not permanently disabled. Furthermore, he considered that her treatment had been conservative. He recommended specific treatment of the injured area with cortisone injections, to be followed by surgery if the cortisone were ineffective. His advice was not followed.

COMMENTS OF SUPERVISOR AND FELLOW EMPLOYEES

The Human Resources Manager of the company began a review of the claim after receiving word of the award. The laboratory supervisor was asked what she thought about the situation. She stated that she had maintained a fairly good relationship with Janice, as she had with all of the other laboratory technicians for that matter, and that Janice was well liked by all. She recalled that, in July, the other technicians were upset after Janice reported having problems. They were upset, not as might be expected, out of sympathy for Janice, but for the increased work load they would need to carry. As the time passed, however, with Janice away from work without a replacement, most of their disenchantment was forgotten, although jokes were passed among the technicians as to which of them would be the next victim.

The laboratory technicians were also asked informally by their supervisor whether they had been having problems performing their work. All denied having any experience similar to that of Janice. They noted, however, that after her vacation Janice seemed to complain about opening sample jars, working under fume hoods with outstretched arms and reaching to set up glassware. All agreed that from time to time this type of work activity was cumbersome, perhaps involving some mild discomfort which usually vanished as quickly as it appeared, but none found it debilitating nor could they identify any tasks leading to lasting or prolonged discomfort. No one was willing to talk openly about a co-worker whom they described as a friend, even if they had their suspicions. Prior to Janice's absence and since, there have been no similar health complaints reported to the supervisor.

The supervisor added another personal observation about Janice, namely, that Janice's work performance began to deteriorate in early February, just after she returned to work following a hysterectomy, although considerably before the onset of the current complaint.

ASSIGNMENT

You've been hired by the company to help prepare a brief for presentation to the panel which reviews disputed claims for workers' compensation.

Given what you know about the facts of this case, as well as the hearsay and the type of work, what is your opinion about the validity of this claim? Would you suggest that the company proceed to contest it, and if so what is your rationale for so doing?

THE LITIGIOUS LAB TECH SOLUTION

In all probability the company has good reason to doubt the validity of this claim, not the injury, but the cause of the injury which most likely took place off the job. The occurrence of the injury as described is not compatible with the type of work performed. An injury such as epicondylitis may occur from the repetitive motions of extension and flexion, or rotation, at the elbow under load, and often to extremes of joint capacity, such as experienced when using a screwdriver, or for that matter playing tennis (hence tennis elbow). The ergonomic precursors of this type of injury, however, are simply not present in the job. If this was a manual, labor-intensive job, or a job involving the use of small tools, or the result of sports activity, then damage to the elbow would be more likely. However, the likelihood of overuse of the elbow joint in this lab tech job is very limited. The actions of opening jars, reaching to clamp glassware, stretching to adjust instrumentation and so on would probably be painful to an already injured elbow, but the issue is whether or not these and other job activities are the cause of the injury. Under the circumstances, this is unlikely.

In disputing the claim, however, the company must mount a convincing case to show a mismatch between the type of injury and the type of work, that is, between the cause and the effect. The argument could be built around the following points:

1. Janice has worked for 15 years without a problem. Chronic work-related problems may take months or even years to develop, but they usually have a discernible history of work-related absenteeism and gradual progression. The rapid onset and lack of history in this case do not fit the expectations.

2. Janice reported her injury shortly after returning from a vacation during which she was assisting her husband in renovating her house, while presumably using small tools. Prior to this vacation she had never reported any work-related injury. She could have sustained the injury during her vacation.

3. The Physical Demands Analysis of the tasks previously described does not support the position of a work-related injury. The necessary repetitive work elements under load to extremes of joint movement are absent from the tasks concerned.

4. Other technicians with similar background in identical jobs remain healthy and present no complaints.

5. While the medical opinions are divergent, more weight should be given to the opinion of the occupational medical specialist. By virtue of training and experience this specialist is more knowledgeable about work conditions and the relationship between work and disability.

It might be noted as an aside that while the type of repetitive strain or overuse injury of the wrist known as carpal tunnel syndrome may be more common in women after the menopause, the injury under consideration is clearly not a carpal tunnel syndrome. Consequently, while the supervisor's comment about Janice's reduced performance after hysterectomy may be interesting, it is irrelevant to the current considerations.

There is no dispute about the fact of the injury. Janice certainly had a severe injury and a possible long-term disability. But while one may have sympathy for the worker, in this case the company cannot be held responsible for its causation and hence the claim should be rejected.

Case VIII

THE SURLY SUPERVISOR

BACKGROUND

David Moody is not a happy man. And he thinks he has lots of reason to be unhappy, for nothing ever seems to be going right. David is forty-seven years old and lives on the outskirts of the city just off the end of the main east-west runway of the International Airport. In fact, he was one of the first persons to buy a house when a housing development opened there some twelve years ago. He bought the house because it was within a mile of his work. He likes to walk to work, despite the road traffic which has become increasingly heavier, although he was a keen motorcyclist in his twenties and thirties. He still uses a motor cycle on occasion, and for the last 15 years he has always worn a safety helmet when motor cycling.

For twenty-five years David has worked for a company that makes wheel rims for cars and trucks. Twenty-two of these years were spent on the main floor tending one or other of the huge presses which form the sheet steel into the shape of a wheel, but for the last three years he has been in the supervisory ranks and now has a little cubicle office in which he does his paperwork. The office, however, is no executive suite. It consists of 120 square feet of floor space carved out of the main floor and surrounded by walls made of 2 × 4's and half-inch plywood, with a ceiling of residential ceiling tile. Two of the 9 ft walls are penetrated by windows, each 2 × 3 ft and glazed with double-diamond glass. A third wall is penetrated by a door which is generally open. The fourth wall is the outer wall of the building made of concrete and galvanized steel. The floor of the office, like the floor of the building, is concrete and, in fact, is continuous with the building floor.

Inside the office are a desk with a telephone and lots of paperwork, two chairs, and a couple of filing cabinets. It is, in fact, this telephone that gives rise to some of Mr. Moody's unhappiness. As far as he's concerned it always seems to be ringing, and every time he picks it up

101

there seems to be someone complaining—the Boss looking for more production, the Union talking about a grievance, Personnel concerned about absenteeism, or something else unpleasant. On top of that, it has been increasingly more difficult for him to make out what people are saying on the telephone. The noise in the plant is bad enough, but it seems that the telephone isn't as clear as it used to be, and although he has complained about it, and it has been checked by the telephone company, things haven't improved. In fact, David is beginning to dread the telephone and is becoming seriously worried about his effectiveness as a supervisor.

It is possible, indeed, that he wasn't the best choice as a supervisor in the first place. He knows the job and always gets his paperwork done in time, but he doesn't handle people well, perhaps because he doesn't always understand what they are saying, particularly in his later years with the company. And recently, over the last few months, he has been becoming more and more withdrawn and less willing to discuss anything with the employees. He was always a worrier, particularly about his health, although surprisingly, and in spite of his worries, his health has always been pretty good. About the worst thing he had was a case of the measles when he was a child, with some complications which left him with a small perforation in the upper left quadrant of his right eardrum.

To add to his troubles he is having difficulty with the Union. Actually, it is not David in particular who is having difficulty with the Union. It is top management. But top management in turn keeps after him to suggest what they should do about it. As far as the workers are concerned the trouble is not the pay, it is the working conditions, and specifically the level of plant noise. David, however, who was a strong Union man for twenty years, has a secret sympathy with their complaints and finds himself torn between the desire of the company to reduce expenditures and the demands of the workers to reduce noise.

THE PROCESS

Virtually all of the manufacturing activity takes place in one large 600 ft × 900 ft open room, that has a concrete floor, 30 ft galvanized steel walls set on a 3 ft concrete plinth and a truss-supported steel V-roof mounted on pillars.

The process is semi-automated. Sheet steel 1/4" stock, which is kept in piles in one corner of the plant on pallets of 50 pieces, each piece 48" ×

36″, is picked up as required by fork truck and carried to the shearing machines. Two workers collaborate to lift each piece on to a shearing machine which cuts it into 12″ strips. From the shearing machine each strip is carried by roller conveyor to a forming machine which bends it into a cylinder and spot welds the ends together. The cylinder rolls out of the machine and drops on to a metal channel where it rolls by gravity, bumping and clattering into the first of a series of large hydraulic presses. In sequence, passed from one machine to another by gravity or roller conveyors, the cylinder is beaten and battered into shape, using cold and hot forming processes, and is welded to other parts as appropriate, until finally a completely formed steel car or truck wheel rolls out of the last machine into a metal bin. The bins, the rejects, and the scrap are then collected by forklift trucks and emptied into containers or stacked as required. Each machine is tended by one or more workers.

The noise is, in fact, intense. Audio communication for the unfamiliar is possible only by shouting in one's ear, although surprisingly the veteran workers seem to communicate without too much difficulty. Although so far the plant has missed undergoing any government inspection, since it is relatively small, all the floor workers have worn cotton wool inserts in their ears since implementation of government regulations some years previously. In fact, one of David's responsibilities is to ensure that these inserts are worn. Even he wears them when he is out on the floor.

The plant manager, who fancies himself as an industrial engineer, although he is not so qualified, took a reading once on a borrowed sound level meter near the center of activities and found it to be 104 dBA. The level in David's cubicle with the door open was 98 dBA, and with the door shut it was 95 dBA, but since the manager was not sure about what the "A" meant he was not clear on how to interpret the reading. To complicate the issue, one of his associates said the reading should have been made in L_{eq}, although he didn't know what it was, and still another said one reading was no good anyway. At this point the manager gave up and decreed that all the floor employees would wear cotton wool inserts which the company would provide.

Be that as it may, David Moody is also having trouble at home. For some years, anyway, and certainly since the last of his kids left home about three years ago, he and his wife haven't been seeing eye to eye, perhaps aggravated by the fact that this period coincided with an increase in his responsibilities at the plant. However, one way or another, with his wife complaining that even when she speaks to him he never pays her any attention, he has found himself retreating to his den where he can spend a couple of hours with his stereo. But even that doesn't seem to satisfy him anymore, and despite his ministrations the speaker system seems to be losing its high frequency response, and anyway his wife is always yelling at him to turn the thing down.

Eventually, feeling run down, out of sorts, suffering from recurrent headaches and sleeping difficulties, as well as chest pains, nausea, loss of appetite and trouble with his digestion, David is ready to quit. He decides to visit the doctor. The doctor, after eliciting a long history of his complaints and concerns, and after giving David a careful examination, tells him that he is suffering from stress associated with the responsibilities of his work. Because of his perforated eardrum, however, he sends him for an audiogram, the result of which is shown in Figure VIII-1.

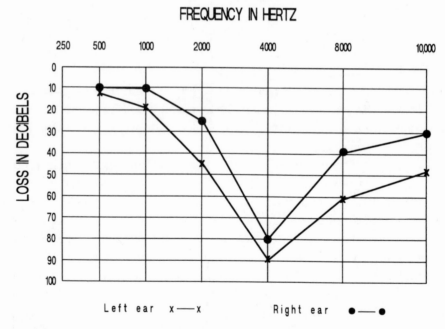

Figure VIII-1. Audiogram of supervisor. Note deep notch at 4000 Hz, which by itself is almost diagnostic of deafness from excessive noise exposure.

ASSIGNMENT

Discuss the situation outlined above using the following questions as a basis for your discussion, as well as other comments that come to mind.

1. Although you may not be a doctor, do you agree with the doctor's diagnosis? Is there anything you can add to it? Explain your decisions and make any other suggestions you consider appropriate.

2. What, if anything, is the significance of his medical history and his life-style?

3. What, if anything is the significance of the perforation in his right eardrum?

4. How is it that some of the veteran workers can communicate without much difficulty, even in the presence of the noise?

5. What physical factors in the plant alleviate or aggravate his noise exposure?

6. What is the significance of the manager's sound level reading? In particular, what are the A, B, and C scales, what is meant by the term L_{eq}, and which, if any, of these measures should be used on this occasion?

7. What are Damage Risk Criteria, and how might they be applied here?

8. What protective equipment might be useful in these circumstances? How effective would the cotton wool inserts be?

9. What should be done about David, now and in the future?

THE SURLY SUPERVISOR SOLUTION

The problem here is clearly one of noise exposure, aggravated by stress induced by the responsibilities of Mr. Moody's job. Noise exposure is too large a subject to discuss in detail. Furthermore, without much more detailed information about the plant layout and noise levels in specific areas it is not possible to state categorically what should be done to bring the noise exposure in this plant to acceptable levels. Accordingly, discussion will be confined to comments on each of the questions that was posed as follows:

Diagnosis

The doctor of course is correct in his diagnosis, as far as it goes. David Moody most certainly is under severe stress, but it should be obvious that he is also suffering from deafness, or more correctly noise-induced permanent threshold shift (NIPTS), and probably has been so suffering for many years. The characteristic severe shift in hearing threshold shown in his audiogram around 4000 Hz is virtually diagnostic. Subjectively, however, his deafness is also indicated by his difficulties in communication with other persons, and particularly with his wife, as well as his problems with telephone and his stereo.

Medical history and life-style

As noted, the doctor concluded that David was suffering from stress. There is no doubt, of course, that he is. He has stress in his relations with management; he has stress in his relations with the Union, and he has stress in his relations with his wife. On top of that, he either always had been, or had become, very unsure of his own abilities, a situation that is aggravated by the increasing deafness of which he seems to be largely unaware. It is also true that continued exposure to noise such as that found in the plant would constitute a stress in itself and certainly would

106

aggravate any other stress effects already present, although noise at the level recorded would not be directly responsible for the other symptoms reported by David. For noise to be the direct cause of nausea, chest pains, and so on, the exposure has to be in the range of about 130–140 dB or more, a range which cannot be tolerated for more than a few seconds.

The perforation of his eardrum is of interest, although really somewhat of a red herring. Perforation of an eardrum is not an uncommon complication of a severe ear infection of the type which can occasionally accompany measles. Curiously, however, a small perforation in the upper left quadrant of the drum is anatomically located in such a position that it gives rise to little or no damage to the bony linkages that transfer vibration of the drum across the middle ear to the inner ear, nor does it interfere with the capacity of the drum to vibrate in response to a stimulus. Consequently, a small perforation in that position has no effect on hearing.

Nor is it likely that his life-style had much in the way of adverse effect on his hearing. There is, for example, no evidence to suggest that recreational motor cycling causes significant noise exposure, particularly when the operator is wearing a safety helmet. The fact that David lives at the end of the runway also has little or no significance, although this might add to his sleeping difficulty and aggravate or compound the stresses already existing. There is no doubt that aircraft on takeoff and landing emit excessive noise. The noise, however, is sporadic, not continuous, and the exposure, while it may be annoying and pose a significant nuisance, is not hazardous. On the other hand, it is possible, although unlikely, that his stereo could be a source of hearing loss, or at least contribute to the hearing loss he acquired at work. There is no doubt that continuous 8-hour exposure to a speaker churning out 40 or more watts of power can present a hazard. However, it is unlikely that he operates it continuously at full volume, and the two hours that he may spend, even if it occurs every night, is unlikely to make much difference, since it is unlikely to approach the excessively high sound levels of work.

Physical factors

The source of the noise is clearly the machinery within the plant. Details of the actual machines in use, their noise-producing characteristics, their shock-mountings if any, and the plant layout are not given in the case study. It can be reasonably assumed, however, from the description of bumping, clattering, difficulties of communication, and indeed from the statement that "the noise . . . is intense," that the noise exposure to the workers tending the machines is above acceptable levels. Indeed, from the text it can be inferred that many, if not all, of the veteran workers have greater or lesser degrees of deafness, since they communicate without too much difficulty. This situation can occur when the persons concerned all have threshold shifts in the same frequency range. They learn unconsciously to interpolate the missing frequencies.

The physical structure of the plant would also have considerable bearing on the noise distribution. The concrete floor and the steel walls would encourage reverberation of the noise generated. The data are not available to determine the extent of that reverberation. It may also be inferred that, because of the nature of the machinery, much of the noise generated would be impact noise. Impact noise may be more damaging than continuous noise.

Although David's cubicle may give him a little privacy, it clearly wouldn't do much for his hearing protection, the less so when the door is open, as it so often is. On top of that, of course, he wears his inserts only when he is on the shop floor although he would still be exposed to excessive noise while in his cubicle.

Sound level measurement

It was fortuitous that the manager made his random measurement of sound pressure level using the A scale. And while his reading may have been neither accurate nor properly done, it does provide an indication of the sound levels in the plant and in the cubicle. The A scale, of course, is one of three electrical circuits, or weighting networks, A, B, and C, which are built into the meter to modify the output before it is displayed. The human ear does not hear sounds with the same intensity at all frequencies. The A scale applies a weighting to the lower frequencies which has the effect of displaying the sound level as it would be perceived by the human ear. The B and C scales, respectively, modify the *raw* noise input with less and less weighting and are used for purposes other than measuring personal noise exposure. For legal purposes, all industrial sound level measures are made using the A scale.

The L_{eq}, or Equivalent Noise Level, is a measure applied to conditions of time-varying noise, and represents the average level of sound energy over a given period of time. It is calculated from repeated measures taken over a given period of time. It is not applicable here. Other measures might have been made with a noise dosimeter, a device which is worn on the person and records the amount of noise to which a person is exposed during, for example, a working day.

Damage risk criteria

The term Damage Risk Criteria is applied to those recommendations, regulations, or laws which prescribe permissible exposure levels and durations of noise exposure. Most legislations recommend, or decree, that industrial exposures should be limited to 85–90 dBA for an 8-hour day, 40-hour week, with other provisions. Many authorities, today, are recommending that the exposure levels be reduced still further, to as low as 80 dBA.

Protective equipment

Noise protective equipment comprises earplugs or inserts, ear muffs, and helmets. Earplugs or inserts can be a valuable asset in a noise protection program. There are many types, varying from inserts of simple cotton batting with an attenuation capacity of about 3–5 dB, to plugs made of firm rubber or plastic which are custom-moulded to fit the individual ear. A good quality plug, inserted and properly fitted, and under controlled laboratory conditions, can give a noise attenuation of 15–23 dB, with the higher levels of attenuation being found at frequencies below 1000 Hz. Since the only inserts worn in the situation described were made of cotton batting, they would not be very effective and certainly would not meet the Damage Risk Criteria. A properly worn earplug, however, is not very comfortable for long periods. It is, of course, the responsibility of a supervisor, such as David, to ensure that employees know how to use ear inserts and that not only are they worn at all times during exposure, but also that they are being properly worn and not merely being stuck loosely into the ear as so often may happen. Ear muffs are even more effective, although sometimes considered clumsy by the wearer. A properly worn ear muff will provide attenuation of 20–40 dB at frequencies above 1000 Hz. Below 1000 Hz its attenuation is similar to that of earplugs. It is probable that ear muffs would be much more effective in this situation than earplugs. A protective helmet can provide attenuation of 50–60 dB. The use of protective equipment is secondary, of course, to the need to reduce the noise at the source.

What to do with David

David should be removed immediately from the noisy workplace and sent for a hearing evaluation by a noise specialist. He should stay away from noise for a period of weeks or even months, according to the recommendation of the specialist, until it can be established what degree of recovery he may achieve, if any. What happens then is open to some controversy. Some authorities consider that when a person suffers severe hearing impairment which is unlikely to be worsened by further exposure, he may return to the noisy environment. Most authorities, however, consider that a worker, even with permanent and severe damage which is unlikely to be further affected, should not be permitted to return to a noisy environment. The decision here would have to be guided by specialist recommendations and workers' compensation guidelines.

Case IX

THE SEATED SORTER

Sally Rodriguez is a postal clerk. She sorts letters in a post office sorting plant. She is forty-four years old, married, and has two children who work in another postal division. She has worked as a sorter for twenty years, as one of fifty-two employees in this particular unit, of whom fourty-two are female. Many of the workers, including Sally, are first or second generation immigrants. They vary in age from twenty-two to fifty-eight. From an anthropometric point of view, that is, in terms of bodily dimensions, Sally is fairly typical of many of her coworkers. She is 152 cm tall and weighs 58 kg. Her standing *high grip reach,* that is, her forward reach with the arm raised some 30 degrees from the vertical, is 175 cm, and her seated high grip reach is 140 cm. Her *reach radius,* that is from the point of the shoulder to the tip of the thumb, is 58 cm.

Like all the other hourly workers, Sally is a member of the local postal union. The union is a national organization and is very influential in determining such matters as wage rates, hours of work, holidays, vacations, and conditions of work. Union/management relations, however, are not of the best and there is a large amount of perhaps justifiable mutual distrust. To compound the difficulties, of recent years management has been trying to operate at a profit in the face of almost insurmountable obstacles. This demand has placed increasing loads upon the employees, to the extent that they have lost some of the privileges that they might previously have enjoyed.

THE JOB

Sally's tasks are assigned by her supervisor. She spends about 90% of her time on letter sorting, with occasional forays into the sorting of oversize mail or small packages. Work is conducted in shifts. As a full-time senior worker Sally has the option of working the day shift (which she does) from 8 A.M. to 4 P.M. The other shifts, from 4 P.M. to midnight, and from midnight to 8 A.M., are largely assigned to new or part-time

111

workers. There is a mid-shift break of 30 minutes for lunch, which is taken in a lunch room equipped with food and drink dispensers, and a 10-minute break in the middle of each half shift, which can also be taken in the lunch room. Employees may not leave their work stations on other occasions except by permission of the supervisor.

The object, of course, is to take the incoming unsorted mail and organize it by geographical region for onward distribution. A series of sorting procedures may be required in different locations in the plant as mail is organized by country, region, city and so on, right down to the level at which it is prepared for local delivery. The actual procedures will be described later.

THE WORK STATION

Sally works in front of a letter sortation case, which is one of a line of such cases at which other employees are doing the same job. Each case comprises rows and columns of pigeon holes into which letters are deposited. Each pigeon hole represents a destination. Letters are deposited therein according to the address on the letter. The case at which Sally works is rectangular in shape and flat in front. It has ten rows by nine columns of pigeon holes, to a total of ninety. It stands on its own supports 65.4 cm above the floor. Projecting from the front at the lowest row is a ledge which slopes slightly upwards from the bottom row to a distance 371 mm in front of the case. This ledge is used for the placement of mail during sorting. The top of the case is 179.1 cm in height above floor level. The case is 149.2 cm in width (Fig. IX-1).

The cases are laid out next to each other forming a series of parallel lines, with the length of the lines being dependent on need and available space, commonly eight to ten per line with one sorter at each. Normally, there is a working space of four metres between two lines, although some of this may be occupied by carts and containers of various kinds holding sorted or unsorted mail.

WORK PROCEDURES

The work routine for Sally is divided into two major parts. The first part, lasting some ten to fifteen minutes, is concerned with organizing her work station and setting up the mail. During this period she obtains string-tied bundles of mail from a nearby bin and loads them on to the

Figure IX-1. There are many different types of postal sorting cases. One in common use, also used by Sally, is illustrated here. It comprises a box with ninety pigeonholes, arrayed in ten rows by nine columns.

ledge in front of her sortation case. The second part is actual sorting, which comprises some seven hours or more. These hours are broken up somewhat randomly to a total of thirty to forty-five minutes, by such tasks as removing letters from full pigeonholes, tying them in bundles and placing them in a container for further distribution, or occasionally collecting a further supply of letters. They are also broken up by coffee and lunch breaks.

When Sally first came to work, all sorting was done from a standing position. For many years she stood on the bare concrete floor when working, but in later years a "fatigue mat" was provided for each of the workers. The fatigue mat comprises a rubber composition mat about 100 cm long by 50 cm wide by 20 mm thick. Some workers indeed manage to acquire two on which to stand.

When sorting from a standing posture she stands in front of the case, approximately in the middle. The front of the ledge is about mid-thigh position. She stoops to select a handful of letters, and then with her preferred hand, which in her case is the right, she places a letter in the appropriate pigeonhole, holding the bundle in her other hand. Because of excessive reach demands, particularly at the upper corners of the case, she moves forwards, backwards, or sideways, and stretches upwards, sometimes on tiptoe, or downwards, to improve the reach. (Taller persons, particularly male, may find a problem in reaching the lower corners from a standing position without bending and twisting their back.) When one bundle is sorted she selects another, and so on throughout the day.

About two years ago, under pressure from the union, who claimed that prolonged standing was a serious threat to health and well-being, management undertook to provide stools for the workers. Workers were required to sit on the stools during the sorting procedures. Standing was not permitted. The stool supplied is a four-legged metal stool with a round, hard unpadded top. The legs are telescopic and may be adjusted a few centimeters by using a screwdriver. Any adjustments to the height are carried out by maintenance personnel upon request from the sorter. The height of the stool at the midpoint of the adjustment is 75 cm above floor level. There is also a metal ring around the lower part of the legs, some 25 cm above floor level. The diameter of the seat is 35.5 cm. Many workers put makeshift pads on the seats.

When sorting from a seated position Sally places the stool in front of the sortation case in the middle. She commonly sits sideways to the case because of the ledge, placing her feet on the ring of the seat, or on a makeshift footstool, or sometimes on the ledge itself (which is forbidden), or on some of the supporting structure of the case (Fig. IX-2). Letters are again brought to the case from the bin and sorted in the same manner as in standing. The upper reach problem, however, is grossly aggravated, to the extent that a sorter may have to raise off the stool, and crouch balanced on the ring, to reach the appropriate box, or more commonly, collect letters intended for the upper corners and place them on the ledge for future sorting (Fig. IX-3).

Management continued the use of the stools for about two years. During that period a productivity study was conducted which showed that productivity, in terms of numbers of letters processed, was reduced by eight percent. Accordingly, twenty-six months after their installation, the stools were removed and employees were required to return to a standing operation, a move which was received with great dismay by the workers.

Figure IX-2. Because of the structure of the case, the sorter is forced to sit slightly sideways, often with one foot on the supporting member or the storage ledge of the case.

COMPLAINTS

Most of the sorters complain of physical ailments induced by their work. A questionnaire study was conducted by the union to determine the extent of these complaints. The questionnaire was prepared by a union consultant. The employees were briefed on how to complete it by union representatives who subsequently handed out the questionnaires and then collected them on completion. Several employees complained of multiple symptoms. The findings can be summarized as follows (Table IX-I):

Several employees complained of multiple symptoms. During Sally's pregnancies, while she was a sorter, she suffered from varicose veins. Although her varicose veins improved to some extent after her pregnancies they never disappeared, and indeed worsened over the later years. She claims they improved during the seated operation, but she has no written medical evidence to justify that claim. She has chronic swelling of her ankles, legs, and feet, with aching in her ankles and calves, as well

Figure IX-3. Because of the dimensions of the sortation case, a sorter normally cannot reach the upper corners from a seated position.

as flattened metatarsal arches and aching in her feet, chronic lower backache, and recurrent tendonitis in the right wrist. These claims are supported by a written reports from her doctor, although the clinical findings are not detailed. It might be noted that, by union agreement, there is no health service in the plant other than First Aid and that the only medical records available are statements of fitness for work supplied by a patient's doctor, which of course do not include clinical evidence or diagnoses unless requested by the patient.

On the grounds that management, by removing the stools from the workplace, has contravened a union agreement pertaining to health and safety, and in so doing has grossly aggravated physical ailments caused originally by her prolonged standing while at work, Sally has filed a grievance with the post office. The grievance is supported by the union who point out that in the union agreement there is a statement to the effect that management will take all measures necessary to maintain health and well-being of the employees while at work.

Table IX-I
MEDICAL COMPLAINTS MADE BY POSTAL SORTERS
AND ATTRIBUTED BY THEM TO THEIR WORK

Type of Complaint	Number of Complaints	Number who Support Seating
Aching and/or pain		
Upper back	18	15
Lower back	42	40
Neck	40	35
Shoulder	45	30
Arm	18	16
Wrist	23	20
Hand	12	10
Thighs	2	2
Calves	31	30
Ankles	38	36
Feet	47	45
Swelling in legs/knees	34	31
Abdominal/digestive problems	5	0
Varicose veins	10	10
Other	15	15

Note: Total number of persons queried: 52

ASSIGNMENT

As a consultant ergonomist called in by management, you are to prepare a report on the relative merits of sitting and standing while at work, with particular application to Sally's problems and the circumstances found in this situation. You are to make appropriate recommendations to management. Management, however, has insisted that any suggested changes must be possible with minimal change to the existing work framework and equipment inventory.

THE SEATED SORTER SOLUTION

The foregoing case outlines various problems, but the problem to be considered here is that of seated versus standing operations. Although a number of internal studies have been conducted by post offices throughout the world, information on postal sorting problems in the open literature is rather sparse. In particular, there is very little if anything comparing seated and standing operations. However, although the sources are not specifically quoted here, there is no doubt that while postal sorting, whether seated or standing, is relatively sedentary work, it can give rise to aching and pain in the neck, back, upper limbs, and legs among many workers, leading in some instances to disabling musculo-skeletal injuries. In some workers it can cause swelling of the ankles and contribute to the cause or aggravation of varicosities. In a few, who perhaps have had pre-existing pathology, it may be a factor in the development of other forms of circulatory disorder.

In this regard it is pointed out that the questionnaire study presented in the body of the case should be accepted with some reservations. You will note that it was designed by a union consultant and distributed and collected by union representatives. These union representatives also instructed the employees how to complete it. Although it indeed confirms the medical complaints that can arise in postal sorting, you should remember that the union and employees, who are at odds with management, might have an axe to grind in presenting it. In particular, they might have wished to show that a seated operation is less harmful than a standing operation. This possible bias is illustrated by some of the findings. For example, while it is physiologically rational that lower backache, aching in the lower limbs, and swelling of the ankles would be relieved by sitting, there is no rational expectation that a seated posture would relieve aching in the arms, wrist, and hand.

It has long been an ergonomic principle that seated work is preferable to standing. This, however, is not always so, particularly if the seating is prolonged and if the seating causes or increases problems of itself. In

118

considering seated versus standing posture for letter sorting, there are three factors that bear specific attention, namely, reach, physiological postural demands, and fixity of position.

Reach

If you look at an ergonomic reference book (see the anthropometric tables in Appendix 1), you will find a wide variation in reach by stature, age, gender and ethnic group. For example, the forward grip reach distance of the 5th percentile U.S. female without excessive stretch is 655 mm for 19- to 25-year olds and 645 mm for 45- to 65-year olds, while that of the 5th percentile Hong Kong Chinese female is 580 mm. These distances are of course *static* reaches, in the horizontal plane with the body held erect. In practice, the worker takes advantage of movement, so that the actual reach also depends on the extent of the body bending and leaning. The reach distance also depends on whether the required reach is in the centerline of the horizontal plane, or above, or below, or off to one side. The functional forward reach and grasp of a 5th percentile Caucasian operator in the centerline at a height of 1500 mm (i.e. lower than the top of the sortation case) is about 500 mm, while at 70 mm to the side of the centerline, or approximately half the width of the case at that height, it is about 140 mm. Thus a standing sorter has problems with the top and bottom rows, and particularly the corners. A tall sorter has less problem with the top rows and more with the bottom. Similarly, the forward functional reach of a 5th percentile operator seated facing an operation is about 250 mm at a height of 1500 mm in the centerline of the horizontal plane. Although the reach to the lower rows is easier for the seated worker, the reach to the higher rows, and particularly the corners, becomes impossible. Remember, also, that a sorter does not sit directly facing the case but sits sideways to it, a posture which favors reach to the near side but not to the off side.

Postural Demand

Two types of muscle work can be defined, namely, static and dynamic. Static work occurs when a muscle is maintained in prolonged contraction, as when you hold your arm out in front of you. Dynamic work occurs when there is a rhythmic contraction and relaxation of muscles, as for example in moving your arm backwards and forwards. Prolonged static work obstructs the blood supply to the muscles while dynamic work encourages it. Consequently, static work is more fatiguing than dynamic.

The act of standing requires a large amount of static work in the muscles of the back, legs, neck and shoulders with resulting aching and pain in these muscles if the standing is prolonged. Seating for rest periods relieves some of the problems of the legs and lower back. It does not relieve upper back and shoulder ache. Furthermore, prolonged seating can give rise to a new set of back problems, as described in the next paragraph.

The vertebrae of the back are separated by discs which act as shock absorbers. A disc comprises a tough fibrous outer ring filled in the center by a membrane which encloses a viscous fluid (the nucleus). The disc can absorb water into the nucleus, the amount of water depending on the vertical force that is being exerted on the spine. Thus during sleep, when the body is horizontal, the disc will swell; during standing, sitting, and postural movements, the water content will be reduced. Furthermore, as a result of back posture, the disc will change its shape and its internal pressure, tending to protrude outwards. Increased pressure and protrusion tends to give rise to pain and aching, and, if sufficiently severe, may cause damage to the nerve fibers emerging from the spinal cord which is located within the vertebrae. Indeed, although not common, the disc may rupture under sudden load with catastrophic results to the back.

Measurements of pressure within the nuclear disc have shown that, compared to the pressure at a nominal 100% in the standing posture, a person seated erect generates a pressure of 40% more, or 140%, a person seated slumped forward generates 90% more, while a person lying down generates only one-quarter of the nominal pressure. The explanation lies in the dynamics of the spinal curvature. In a seated position only 60 degrees of the bend derives from the hip joints; the other 30 degrees come from flattening the normal forward facing curve in the lumbar portion of the spine. This in turn causes the disc to be deformed into a wedge shape with an increase in the internal pressure. It will be apparent, then, that prolonged seating, although acting in a different manner, may be just as uncomfortable, and indeed disabling, as prolonged standing, although it may take longer before the discomfort becomes apparent.

Fixity of position

The third factor to be considered is fixity of position. As is well known to anyone who has travelled for a prolonged period seated in an aircraft, being fixed in one position tends to increase gravity-dependent swelling, particularly in the ankles. The muscle action which takes place during movement tends to act as a pump to return the blood to the heart. In standing, unless forcibly maintained as in standing to attention, it is common to shift one's weight from one leg to the other, move one's feet, and so on, the more so if the nature of the task is conducive to some motion. In a seated position, adjustment is more difficult, and postural adjustments, where feasible, tend to be more gross, perhaps requiring actual movement in or off the seat.

Both sitting and standing in one position for prolonged periods gradually produce intolerable discomfort. Indeed, in one study of office workers, it was observed that workers continually adjusted their position in various areas of the seat — on the front edge, in the middle, towards the back, leaning on the backrest, or supporting their arms on a table. Wherever feasible, seated workers will stand up, stretch, and readjust themselves before sitting down again. Indeed, if it is possible, workers spend some time standing and some time sitting at the job.

Seats

Factors governing the selection of an appropriate seat for postal sorting are very controversial. Depending on whether the intent is to optimize short-term comfort at the expense of aggravating the reach problem, or to minimize the reach problem at the expense of short-term comfort, a different seat would need to be considered. Workers will prefer a seat that optimizes short-term comfort, perhaps at the expense of productivity. In fact, any shop floor test of a preferred seat will be biased in favor of comfort, so that the use of stools which might be to the long-term advantage of the worker will be dismissed by the workers concerned since they may not be so comfortable.

If comfort is the criterion, then the stool should conform to the ergonomic standards of being easily adjustable in height and seat angle, padded and upholstered in a textured cloth that reduces slippages, with a roll-off at the front to reduce pressure on the back of the thighs. It should have a back rest, adjustable in height and back angle, and perhaps one or two armrests. To ensure stability it should have five legs with a ring around the lower part of the legs which can be used as a footrest.

However, at least as desirable as the design of the seat is the necessity to designate the sorting activity as a sit/stand operation, such that the worker is not required either to sit or stand all the time. If this be the case, then comfort and back support may no longer be the primary criteria in selection of a seat. Consideration should be given to adopting a "perching" seat on which a worker would sit facing the sortation case with one buttock on the front of the seat, one leg one the seat ring, and the other on the floor. In this position he/she can reach most of the pigeonholes with less effort than from a fully seated position, and indeed can shift from one leg and buttock to the other, or even momentarily to the floor. Pressure can still develop on the buttock, but it can be relieved by changing sides. The posture is a compromise, more comfortable than standing, less so than sitting, but it is one that provides a greater extent of reach with no fixity of position.

Health and Well-Being

Sally's grievance was based on a claim that management failed to meet the requirements of ensuring health and well-being. In this connection it is necessary to distinguish between the "normal" discomfort, aching and other symptoms associated with manual work, even sedentary manual work, and the occurrence of impairment or significant pathology. Available statistics are not very helpful.

From the few studies that have been conducted there is no doubt that a standing operation can give rise to discomfort, aching, and even pain. These symptoms in themselves, however, are not evidence of impairment of health. It is only when the symptoms cross the line into pathology that one can say that health has been affected, and, of course, that line may be difficult to determine. One might make a case, however, on the basis of swelling of the ankles, or flattened metatarsal arches, provided that these could be shown not to have existed before exposure to the work conditions, or perhaps had been aggravated by such exposure. Ultimately, the decision might have to be based on the credibility of expert witnesses, one of whom might say the working conditions were responsible, and the other that they were not.

RECOMMENDATIONS

Bearing in mind the above discussion, and the details outlined in the case, the following is presented as a summary of possible recommendations, of which any or all might be desirable depending on conditions and feasibility:

- designate the sorting operation as a sit/stand operation;
- organize and enforce a sit/stand schedule such as two hours standing work and two hours sitting work, with appropriate breaks in between;
- use a perching position on stools rather than a full-seated position;
- provide stools for all workers;
- provide, and enforce the use of, fatigue mats for all situations in which sorting is done while standing;
- develop a system of rotation through different types of work, if feasible, perhaps on a weekly basis;
- reduce the working area of the sortation case, if feasible, by blocking out the peripheral rows and columns, or at least by blocking out corners;
- give consideration to a minor redesign of the sortation case by removing the central one-third of the ledge to allow the sorter greater access to the pigeonholes. Alternatively remove the ledge entirely and replace it with a movable wheeled cart to be placed beside the sorter and also used for collecting mail to be sorted.

Case X

THE SMALL TOOL TELEPHONE TRAUMA

Reconditioned Phones is a company which takes apart old telephones, reconditions them, and sells them for private use, mostly in third-world countries. The telephones that are serviced are of the old type, square-bodied table models made of black metal or plastic. The company has been in business for just under two years and is wholly owned by an international communications corporation.

To do the work the company employs thirty-seven hourly workers. Twenty-seven of the workers are female with ages ranging between twenty-two and forty-five. Of these, twenty are employed in disassembly, replenishing, and re-assembly of the incoming telephones. The remainder are used in various aspects of testing, packaging, and so on, and in clerical duties. The males are employed in maintenance and support roles. By agreement with the parent company, twenty-four of these workers, including all of those involved in disassembly, replenishment and re-assembly, were hired from the parent company because of downsizing and layoff. This case involves the twenty females who are engaged in disassembly, replenishing, and re-assembly. All of the females had previously been employed as telephone operators, or in some form of clerical work. None had ever done manual work using hand tools before. More than half, however, had responsibility for a home and family as well as their work. Several of these, and many of the remainder, also enjoyed active recreation in the form of bowling, exercise activities, dancing, some golf and tennis, and so on.

OPERATIONAL PROCEDURES

While in fact none of the workers underwent any form of medical examination prior to being transferred into this new job, nor was there any form of pre-placement examination for new hires brought in later, none of the workers reported any adverse medical history to the Human Resources department on hiring. No medical facilities other than First

Aid are available at the plant. Any medical complaints at work are reported to the First Aid room, staffed as and when required by Human Resources personnel. If necessary, by agreement with the First Aid staffer and the employee, the complainant is then dealt with on the spot or referred to the hospital or her doctor. Medical certificates indicating fitness for continued work, without any other information, are subsequently received from these sources when required. A log of visits and comments by the First Aid worker is kept in the First Aid room. Medical certificates, supervisors reports, and so on are kept by Human Resources. No medically confidential material is kept.

The plant operates on one shift, from 7:00 A.M. until 3:00 P.M., a shift which is convenient for those with family responsibilities. There is a half-hour break for lunch, taken in a lunch room on the premises, and two fifteen-minute coffee breaks, which can also be taken in the lunch room.

When the company was started, each worker received one day of instruction from time and motion study trainers on what had to be done. Each new worker now receives one day of on-the-job training from an experienced fellow worker. Work stations are assigned by the supervisor on the basis of seniority and according to the worker's choice. There is little difference between the work stations in the disassembly and re-assembly operations. The choice of station is mostly based on congeniality of neighbors.

Payment is calculated on a daily basis. Each employee has a quota of work to be completed in the course of a shift. Bonuses are paid for work over quota and deductions made for work less than quota. Employees are not dissatisfied with this system.

The Work

There are three phases to the work of this particular group. These comprise, firstly, disassembly, in which the telephones are broken down to their subcomponents, cleaned, and where worn parts are removed; secondly, replenishment, where worn and missing parts are acquired, sorted, and laid out for re-assembly; and thirdly, re-assembly, which is self-explanatory.

Disassembly

Incoming telephones are brought to the plant in cardboard cartons, six phones per carton. Prior to the beginning of actual disassembly, the phones are removed from the carton and the black housing is dismantled from each phone. The housing and phone are then placed on a 16" × 12" plastic tray. The tray has a raised 1" edge around it with a sharp rim. The tray containing the phone and housing is then placed on a roller conveyor and slid by gravity on its way to the disassembly line.

The disassembly line consists of a row of identical work stations spaced some two feet apart (Fig. X-1). Each station comprises two sides of a square. The worker sits within the square, facing forward into one side, with the other to her right. The work surface in front of her is 35" above floor level and provides a work area 46" wide by 14" deep. The bench to her right is a similar size. The work surface is covered with green, rubber-backed carpet. There are two storage shelves above the right-hand bench. These are used for parts, cleaning materials, seldom-used tools, and personal storage. The bench is well illuminated by an adjustable, overhead bench light.

Beyond the front work surface are two roller conveyors, one above the other, connecting the various work stations. These are used to bring and remove trays of telephones to and from the work station. The lower conveyor brings the incoming trays, the upper sends the disassembled telephone to the restoration area. The conveyors are 14" wide. Since the system is gravity-fed, the conveyors are at different heights at each work station. At the high end of the line, the upper conveyor is 23" above the work surface; at the low end it is 14"; the lower conveyor runs parallel to the upper, 10" below it (see Fig. X-1).

Scattered over both the benches, generally to the right, is a number of hand tools provided by the company. These comprise 10" and 6" blade screwdrivers with 1/4" and 1/8" blades, respectively, a 10" ratchet screwdriver with a 1/4" blade, a set of Phillips screwdrivers, an X-acto® cutting knife with blades, spring-loaded pliers with a 6" spread at the handles, needle-nosed pliers with a 5" spread, a screw-lifter, a toothbrush, and sundry other scrapers, cutters, fasteners, wipes and cleaners. The screwdrivers have a domed end and hard plastic fluted handles. Some workers privately purchase and add tools of personal preference.

Although the station was designed for a standing operation, stools were introduced shortly after the operation commenced. The worker sits

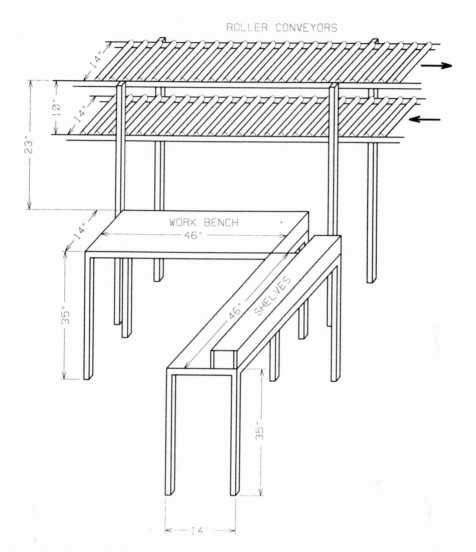

Figure X-1. Telephone disassembly work station showing where the operator is seated facing the roller conveyors. The lower conveyor delivers telephones for disassembly, while the upper is used to dispatch the disassembled telephones to the restoration area.

on a cushioned stool readily adjustable to meet the sitting height of a 90th percentile population. The seat is square, flat and has a cushion 16″ wide, 14″ deep and 3″ thick. The seat is movable on four castors and has a built-in circular footrest 19″ in diameter located 6″ above floor level. The back angle and tension of the seat back frame are adjustable; the lower edge of the back rest is located 5″ above the seat cushion. The back rest swivels in the vertical plane and is 14″ wide by 9″ high with a back curve that is 2″ deep. Although the seat provides relatively little leg room under the bench for an *average* 64″ female and does not permit working with the legs crossed, it is well liked by the workers.

In operation, the worker removes from the lower conveyor a tray containing a telephone and places it on the work surface in front of her. Stabilizing the phone and tray with one hand (normally the left hand of a right-handed person), she detaches and/or cleans any or all, as appropriate, of the handset, the line cord, the finger wheel, the dial plate, and any damaged or corroded parts, resting her forearm on the edge of the tray when her arm is not otherwise raised up. She cleans the interior, removing labels, and wraps and/or otherwise secures the various items. These actions require the repetitive use of a variety of different tools, using a greater or lesser amount of force. Because of her seated position, she spends much of her time working with her back bent sideways, slightly twisted, with one arm resting on the bench holding the tray, and the other raised high at the shoulder and bent at the elbow so that she can manipulate her tools.

If the screws are not too tight, the screwdriver is held in a pinch grip, with the butt of the driver against the palm of the hand. The screw is then removed by a repetitive backward supination and pronation (that is, rotary motion) at the wrist in a right-handed person, while the elbow and shoulder remain more or less fixed. If the screw is sealed or very tight, as many are, the screwdriver is clenched in a power grip around the handle without inverting the hand, that is as one would grasp a pole, and the screw is removed by very forcible repetitive horizontal palmar and dorsiflexion at the wrist with concomitant motion at the elbow and shoulder. Occasionally, the worker will stand and use two hands on the screwdriver. Phones with screws that cannot be loosened are put aside.

The ratchet screwdriver, which is used whenever feasible, has a spherical handle which is grasped in a power grip and operated by repetitive up-and-down flexion at the elbow. The cutters, scrapers and other small tools are tightly grasped in a pinch grip. Some workers wear cloth gloves provided by the company to protect their hands.

Pliers are used to pinch wires and fasteners, removing them with a repetitive twisting and rotary motion at the wrist. Depending on requirement, the pliers may be used in two different configurations. Commonly, the pliers are grasped with the jaws facing upwards and outwards, while using rotary motions at the wrist with the elbow flexed and the upper arm extended at the shoulder. This mode is more forcible than an alternative method where the pliers are grasped with the jaws facing downwards and backwards. In this mode they are operated by way of repetitive palmar and dorsiflexion while the elbow and shoulder remain relatively fixed. Some have difficulty using the large spring pliers in this way because of the excessive finger spread required and the force of the spring.

When disassembly is complete, the worker signs the job off, places the tray containing the telephone and relevant parts on to the upper conveyor, and sends it on down the line to the replenishment stations. A loaded tray weighs approximately 5¼ pounds.

Replenishment

The objective of replenishment is to replace those parts previously removed so that the telephone can be re-assembled. The operation is done from a standing position at the same type of bench. The working floor space is covered with rubber matting. Small parts are stored in containers on two racks resting on the side bench. The racks are three tiers high, with each tier holding four containers. Each container is 4″ wide by 6″ long by 3″ high. The tiers of the racks are 8″ apart and tilted forward to allow easier access to the parts within. Access to the lower tiers from a standing position, however, is still awkward because of interference from the upper tiers. Larger parts are stored in cartons on the floor behind the operator and are piled to a height of 48″ above floor level. Each carton is 25″ wide by 20″ fore and aft by 6″ deep. They are stacked, eight on end, to a height of 48″ above floor level.

In operation the employee takes a tray from the conveyor, scans the tray to identify missing parts, stretches to select parts from the boxes above the conveyor, or turns and bends to select parts from the boxes behind her, and places the parts on the tray before sending it on its way for re-assembly. As the cartons behind her are depleted they are discarded. The working level is thus reduced and the worker has to stoop further to acquire a part.

Re-assembly

Re-assembly is conducted at a work station similar to that for disassembly. It is done in a seated posture. A rack similar to that on the replenishment bench is located on the bench at the worker's side. It is used for storage of screws, fasteners, and so on. Many of the workers consider that re-assembly is less physically demanding than disassembly since there is no requirement to use excessive force for the removal of tight fasteners.

Incoming work arrives on the conveyor at a height of 14″ to 18″ above the bench. The outgoing conveyor lies 10″ below the incoming. The worker places a tray on the bench and, using various small tools, assembles any or all of the following: the ringing mechanism, circuit board, dial and dial parts, hand unit, and line cord. She also cleans and prepares contacts and dial components, and *dresses,* or organizes, the wires. After completing the paperwork she replaces the tray on the outgoing conveyor and sends it on its way. The available tools include a terminal insertion tool, a blade screwdriver, a ratchet screwdriver, a round file, orange sticks, needle-nose pliers, Phillips screwdriver, and an X-acto knife.

THE PROBLEM

Within days or weeks of starting work, employees began to complain of pain and aching in any or all of the wrist, the forearm, the elbow, the neck, the shoulder, and the back, either right or left side depending on whether they were right or left handed. By the end of six months two workers had been off work for over a month each, with a medical diagnosis of tendonitis at the wrist. These workers returned to work after a total of six weeks leave, but were again laid off with the same diagnosis three months later. At the end of the first year five more workers were laid off within a period of two weeks with musculo-skeletal problems involving the wrist and shoulder region. These latter layoffs caused much consternation among the remaining workers. Suddenly five more workers reported with medical certificates stating that they were temporarily unfit for further work because of various musculo-skeletal injuries, bringing the total number of injured workers to twelve, more than half of those engaged in the work.

These unscheduled layoffs have been playing havoc with production, while the job is getting a bad name among potential workers. In addition to their humanitarian concerns, management is also becoming anxious about likely increases in workers' compensation dues. Unfortunately, since there are no medical records other than a few reports in the First

Aid log and the medical certificates held by Human Resources (Personnel), it is difficult to determine the medical extent of the problem.

ASSIGNMENT

As a consultant ergonomist you have been asked by management to review the problem and make a report on what actions might be taken to reduce the sickness absenteeism. Your report should outline your view of the nature of the problem and the causative factors. It should include recommendations on the administrative, engineering, and/or other approaches that might be taken to ameliorate the working conditions.

THE SMALL TOOL TELEPHONE TRAUMA SOLUTION

The problem here is clearly one of intensive use of small hand tools in a seated posture that is not always conducive to the best use of these tools. The problem is aggravated by the fact that prior to beginning this job, the workers had not been exposed to manual labor, even the manual labor of small tool use, and that, furthermore, the quota system in use places a greater demand on them than might otherwise be required. When there is an incentive quota system there is a tendency for workers to work at a much greater than normal intensity during the first part of the shift so that they can ease off in the latter part. This may have the effect of overstressing the muscles and joints during the first part of the shift.

It is medically well established that repetitive motion at joints, often to extremes of movement under load, can give rise to various forms of musculo-skeletal injury known collectively as repetitive strain injury (RSI), or sometimes cumulative trauma disorder, or, more generally, overuse injury. There are various clinical terms applied to these injuries, according to site. For example, when the injury involves the tendons and/or their tendon sheaths around the wrist it is known as tendonitis, or tenosynovitis; when it affects the elbow it is known as epicondylitis, and so on. A particular variety, called the carpal tunnel syndrome, affects the tendons and their sheaths as they pass through a bony and ligamentous tunnel in the lower wrist. That condition can cause sensory and sometimes motor paralysis of the outer fingers of the hand.

These injuries normally give rise to pain and aching during and after the causative work. The pain may become sufficiently severe to limit or even prevent the causative actions, and indeed, if the worker persists in the actions, the resulting injury can lead to a permanent disability. The injury, however, is normally relieved by rest and removal from the causative work for periods of weeks to months. It may recur if the worker is returned to work too soon. The worker should not be returned to work without a period of physical therapy and rehabilitation. In many instances, indeed, the worker should not be returned to the same work that caused the injury unless modifications to that work or workplace have been made.

The classic type of work that can give rise to RSI is one in which the arms are used in a *wringing* action, as in wringing a towel. This type of action is found in using a screwdriver or other kinds of tools that require a rotary motion at the wrist. Since many of the small tools are used in this manner, it is not at all surprising that the workers suffer from RSI. In addition, the fact that the workers are using these tools in a seated posture at a horizontal bench aggravates the problem. Under these circumstances a right-handed worker using a screwdriver, for example, in a normal grip, has to twist the back sideways, raise the right elbow above shoulder height and then use a rotary screwing motion while in that position. This process may be repeated hundreds of times a day while the wrist is rotated perhaps thousands of times. If the screwdriver is grasped in a power grip, then the wrist is flexed and extended hundreds or thousands of times a day, a situation which again produces great stress on the tendons and their sheaths. The fact, also, that the bench is horizontal increases the stress on the elbow and shoulder. If the bench were tilted, the elbow would not have to be raised.

Still other problems arise from the back stretching and arm movements required to reach small parts and tools, from the need to lift trays to and from high conveyors, and from the bending and twisting of the back to acquire larger parts from storage containers.

There is another factor here of interest. You might recall that after the end of the first year, when five workers were laid off with wrist and shoulder problems, suddenly five more workers also reported injuries. Consideration should be given here to the possibility of what has been termed occupational mass hysteria and the role of compensation. This condition can arise when occupational health or injury problems in a plant creep through the whole work force. If the conditions are right, the unaffected workers may begin obsessively noticing otherwise minor personal ailments, to the extent that these minor problems now begin to assume serious proportions among some of the workers, eventually leading to a work stoppage. This can happen very suddenly. Indeed, when toxic conditions are erroneously suspected in the environment, it can happen within minutes.

Clearly, then, there is also a lack of understanding of the nature of the problem both by the workers and by management. Each would benefit from further education, while in addition there are many other steps that might be taken to relieve the situation. In general, these steps can be classified in terms of either administrative or engineering approaches. These will not be presented here in detail, but an outline of some is given below. The outline is not necessarily complete nor is it presented in any order of precedence. Some suggestions are relatively easy to implement; some more complex. Not all will be found acceptable but nevertheless they should be considered. Indeed, much of the management of the problem has to be based on having someone in the company who is familiar with the ramifications of RSI and its control; consequently, one of the first recommendations has to do with the appointment of a part-time occupational health nurse.

RECOMMENDATIONS

Administrative

1. Hire a part-time occupational health nurse (½ to 1 day per week, or more, depending on requirement) for occupational health services and medical record keeping.

2. Develop and implement a confidential medical record system for employees, particularly those with upper limb complaints, using the services of the part-time occupational health nurse. Information should include demographic data, date of reporting, date when injury incurred or became apparent, description or diagnosis, referral if any, treatment if any, date of return to work, rehabilitation requirements, work limitations if any, work or work station modifications if any, and follow up.

3. Conduct a survey, supervised by the occupational health nurse, to determine those jobs and/or tasks most responsible for musculo-skeletal injury.

4. Develop, within the limits of current human rights legislation, pre-placement medical evaluation procedures for newly hired persons and for persons transferred from other divisions to assist in guiding them into the appropriate job.

5. Develop an appropriate form to be completed by personal physicians and returned to the company for those workers who are rendered unfit by reason of musculo-skeletal injury. The form would not include confidential information, but, to the extent feasible, it would include diagnosis, prognosis, cause of injury, and likely duration of absence.

6. Develop liaison with personal physicians to the extent feasible, inviting them to the plant to see the nature of the work being done.

7. Under the control of the occupational health nurse, develop a rehabilitation program for returning workers, and a physical exercise arm-strengthening program for non-injured workers.

8. Initiate educational seminars for management, health and safety committee members (where such committees exist), and lead hands (or the equivalent), outlining the fundamentals of ergonomics as well as the nature and causation of RSI, with particular reference to the conditions on the shop floor, and the potential for mass hysteria.

9. Ensure that supervisors instruct workers on the way to use tools in such a manner as to minimize musculo-skeletal strain, as advised by the ergonomist and/or occupational health nurse. Ensure that supervisors monitor proper usage, and specifically that they do not strain at tightly attached fasteners.

10. Initiate a task training program whereby new employees, transferees, or those returning from rehabilitation are introduced to a task on a graduated basis over a period of not less than five days.

11. Encourage workers to alternate between sitting and standing while working, and in particular to stand when applying force.

Engineering

12. Introduce an air-powered driver on each bench. The driver should be hung on a light spring so that the handle, commonly cylindrical in shape, is about 15″ above bench level. It should be readily accessible for use and should return to resting position on release. It would be wise to cover the handle with a soft vinyl sheath, flanged at the lower end, to improve grasp quality. The driver should require no more than 8 ounces of pressure in operation.

13. Initiate a survey, using established ergonomic principles, to select and provide the most suitable hand tools, for example, bent-handle pliers, pliers sized appropriately to the size of the hand, light springs on pliers rather than heavy, knurled surfaces or rubber-cushioned screwdrivers rather than ridged or flanged, knives with angled and shaped handles, and so on. Provide necessary tools and ensure that no others are used.

14. Replace existing trays with others having lower sides, rolled out-

wards to minimize employee forearm trauma and to increase accessibility to work.

15. Provide non-slip surfaces on benches to minimize relative motion between bench and tray.

16. Raise bench levels at the high end of the roller lines to reduce the stretch. Provide a platform, if necessary, on which to mount the seat.

17. Mount storage cartons in the Replenishment area on a spring jack device to keep them at an optimal level. Tilt them forward to allow easier access.

18. Redesign the storage containers in the Replenishment area to allow easier access to the parts from a standing position.

19. Replace existing stools with "sit-stand" stools so that the new posture of the worker would reduce the required elbow angle and allow easier application of force while using small tools. This recommendation would not be initially well accepted by the workers since it is less comfortable for the legs and lower body, but the sit-stand posture would reduce the stress on elbows and shoulders.

20. Alternatively, at greater expense, tilt the work benches forward to place them at an angle more suitable for work by a seated operator. The bench would then require a jig, moveable to some extent in five degrees of freedom, on which the telephone and components could be mounted; or indeed the jig might replace the tray. The air-driver, other tools and parts, would then have to be relocated.

CASE XI

THE HAITIAN HANDSAW

There is always some fascination with different cultures, their perceptions, and their ways of doing things. This is a case where, to meet the demands of a different culture, one must consider the redesign of an apparently simple tool, the design and usage of which has remained unchanged for centuries. The tool is one we are all familiar with, namely, the simple cross-cut handsaw used for cutting wood. The cultural demand comes from the country of Haiti where workers have adopted what many would consider a most unconventional way of using that tool.

BACKGROUND

Even those of us who are not carpenters, or cannot profess to be handymen, know how to use a saw. We may not be able to describe what we are doing and may not so much as picked up a saw ourselves, but the design and method of use appear to be intuitive to us. We grasp the handle with the preferred hand in what is often called the pistol grip. Starting at the distal end of the cut-line, the cut is worked towards the body. The saw blade, teeth down, oriented diagonally downwards, is drawn back and forth across the wood, pushing forcefully on the downstroke engaging and cutting the wood, tiny fragments being sheared from the main stock, but retracting lightly on the backstroke to free and re-position the blade. With the arm in pendulous motion each stroke is similar to the last almost without exception. Most of the strength and force is provided by the large muscle mass in the upper arm and the shoulder. The forearm and hands glide back and forth on a nearly horizontal track, changing only to effect a deeper cut. To achieve the best mechanical advantage and a good line of sight, the upper body is bent over the cut, a hand, a foot, a knee or the weight of the body stabilizing the wood, holding it and preventing it from sliding (Fig. XI-1).

Haitians are familiar with this technique, but they prefer another. Rarely do they follow the method described except when making a small

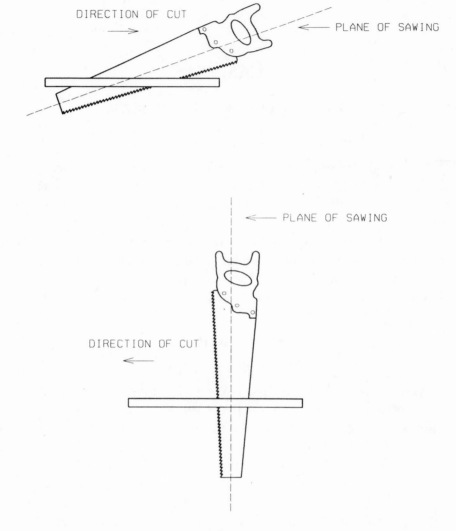

Figure XI-1. Schematic illustrating the basic differences between the two methods of sawing wood. Note the orientation of the saw and the direction of the cut.

cut. Instead, they typically use the saw backwards. Yes! backwards, in almost every way, beginning with the grip (Fig. XI-2). The handle is gripped to allow sawing in the vertical axis, rather than the horizontal. With the saw upright and the teeth oriented away from the body, the cut is made using long upward and downward strokes of the forearm. The saw moves in a natural arch from a near vertical position at the top of the stroke to an oblique angle at the end of the stroke. The circular motion results primarily from flexion and extension at the elbow joint and is illustrated in a series of photos (Figs. XI-3 to XI-11). The action of the forearm is similar to that occurring during hammering, only without the hammering and wrist involvement. The job is sometimes one-handed, but two hands are used to recruit the larger muscle mass in the shoulder when thick pieces of timber are being cut into planks or as fatigue sets in. Figure XI-2 captures both methods in juxtaposition to one another, the conventional method of sawing wood as performed by the person on the left of the photo, the Haitian method on the right.

Cutting is performed from the proximal end to the distal end of the cut-line, working the cut away from, rather than towards, the body. Usually the person stands while cutting. Someone else may hold the wood, or it may be abutted against an obstacle to prevent it from sliding, unless it has sufficient mass to remain steady. Commonly, this method is used for producing planks and for making wooden doors, furniture, and other things.

Why Haitian woodworkers engage in this seemingly unusual art of sawing is a matter of speculation. When asked why they prefer to use this seemingly unorthodox approach, woodworkers simply reply by saying that they find it easier. Comparison of the two methods would make for an interesting biomechanical analysis, but perhaps the Haitians are right. Upon reflection it can be shown that the dynamics of motion are fundamentally different, because sawing as we know it involves the shoulder and upper limb considerably more, whereas the movement is almost exclusively about the elbow joint using the Haitian method.

The series of photos (Figs. XI-2 to XI-11) is intended to give a more graphic representation of the hand tool usage. The photos are taken from a small carpentry shop in Port au Prince, the capital. As is the way in the developing world, there is no *shop* to speak of, just a small workbench at the side of the road where the wares are made, then sold.

Assignment

Comment on why you think this technique has evolved. Assume that the cultural stereotype allows you to change the design of the saw, but not the technique, an assumption that is likely to hold true. What changes would you make to the hand tool to better adapt it to the local usage?

Figure XI-2. The conventional and Haitian methods of using the saw.

Figure XI-3. A typical small carpentry shop in Port au Prince, Haiti. Materials and tools are scant, facilities minimal to the extreme. The only foreign object in the picture is the camera case belonging to one of the authors.

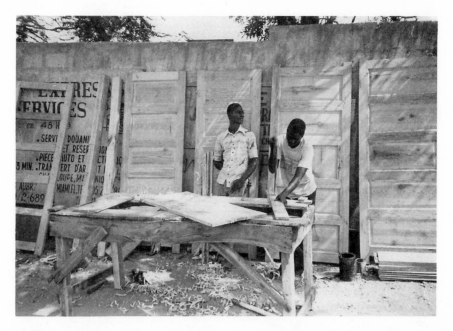

Figure XI-4. This carpentry shop specializes in the manufacture of doors for houses and offices. It employs 3 full-time workers and another 1–2 part-time apprentices. The shop produces only the one product. The wood, a softwood, most likely a Ponderosa Pine, is imported from the United States. In this sequence of photos strips of inlay are being cut to finish the doors.

Figure XI-5. The cutting action commences here near the top of the downstroke. The blade has just been repositioned to begin another stroke as evident by the angle of the blade. Note the teeth and blade are slightly angled into the cut. During retraction the cutting edge of the blade is pulled slightly away and the angle extended away from the wood.

Figure XI-6. The motion of the hand in the sagittal plane forms an arch. As the saw blade moves through the down-stroke, the cutting angle becomes more acute. From the position shown, the blade is approximately at mid-stroke.

Figure XI-7. This photo captures the end of the cutting stroke. Note the oblique position of the blade relative to the wood. See the cutting angle; compare it to the top of the cutting stroke, as shown in Figure XI-5.

Figure XI-8. The worker stands to one side of the piece being cut. Rarely, a worker may position himself directly in line with the cut, the blade passing between the legs as the cut is made. This photo also illustrates that woodworkers generally have no difficulty in following the line of the cut, a question that you might raise. Note the hand grip.

Figure XI-9. This photo shows the saw blade being retracted. Compare this to Figure XI-5 and note the difference. The cutting edge is almost vertically upright.

Figure XI-10. Experienced woodworkers have no difficulty in performing fine cuts. Here, the small strips are being cut diagonally to form the inlay for the doors. The blade is on the upstroke.

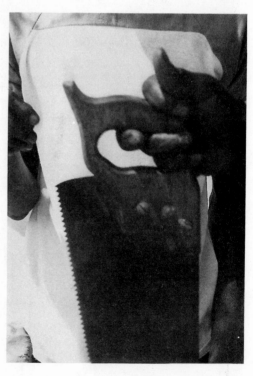

Figure XI-11. A closeup showing the hand grip. This individual is slightly peculiar, in that he prefers to set his thumb on the index finger, which does not show up clearly in Figure XI-10. Most of the woodworkers observed stretch the index finger out over the handle, as shown in Figure XI-8.

THE HAITIAN HANDSAW SOLUTION

Cultural stereotypes and beliefs may seem strange to a foreigner, though the roots of these idiosyncrasies often lie in plausible explanations. Consider this possibility. Experienced laborers manage to tune their performance, to conserve energy, to maximize effort, just as skilled athletes do. Self-selection is a well-known phenomenon amongst our manual labor population, the older experienced workers often representing those who have adopted a successful coping strategy, those who have learned the rule of survival of the fittest in their particular occupation. In a country like Haiti where virtually everything is in short supply, nothing goes to waste. This can be said of almost any materials, food, supplies, resources, etc. The same probably holds true for human energy expenditure.

Speculation has already been raised as to the biomechanical differences between the two methods. Whether one method offers a biomechanical advantage over the other depends upon the relative efficiency of the anatomical leverage systems, the strength capabilities of the corresponding muscle groups and energy expenditure. However, it is instructive to note that Haitian woodworkers are familiar with the method we consider customary. Theirs is a conscious choice to exercise an alternative mode of work. For all we know it might even be a better way. So why do you suppose that Haitians cut wood this way? There are several plausible explanations. No doubt you have some of your own, but here are some speculations.

Although it has a wild history of slavery, conquest, reconquest and dictatorship, Haiti has been relatively isolated from the rest of the developing world, despite its close proximity to the United States. Much that is done in Haiti today is done the same way as it was 300 years ago. It is possible, then, that the use of the saw in the manner described derives from the practices of the old pit saw used by the early colonists and their forebears for making lengthwise cuts in logs. The practice would likely

145

be observed even today if the tree population was not so totally depleted in Haiti, for it is still referred to in the rural communities.

A large pit was created for this purpose, approximately the depth of a man. A log was placed across the pit; one worker stood on the log or on some other nearby structure, holding a long saw in the vertical position; another stood in the pit underneath holding the other end of the saw. Together they worked the saw vertically. One might speculate that the technique continued even when the saw became small and the pit was no longer in use, because this was the way Haitians had learned to saw wood. Yet, this explanation falls short, because our learning followed the same course. Obviously, the advantages of mechanization were not equally shared, which may have been a factor.

Other factors might also play a part. We have the luxury in our society of having access to specialized tools and equipment. Where this access does not exist people are forced to be resourceful, to work with what they have. In Haiti, tools, like most things, are not affordable, nor are they available. To have a saw is to have a trade. No one has a saw unless he considers himself a carpenter. One saw must do the work of all—circular saw, band saw, table saw, and so on. It is possible that only one tool was generally available for cutting; one method came to fit the majority of needs and thus became the accepted way of doing things.

Indeed, the Haitian method is not totally surprising. Examine our own technique for using the power saw and the following will be noticed. Compare the actions of using the hand saw versus the power saw, and you will invariably note that the hand saw and the power saw are generally used in the opposite directions. The hand held power saws, of which there are a few basic types including the circular and jig saws, is pushed away from the body, or in the case of the larger fixed blade band and table saws the wood is pushed towards the blade. Why? because it's easier, there is more control over the cut, and lines and markings can be followed, other safety issues aside.

You may be thinking that there are no obvious parallels and that the skill requirements of the Haitians are quite different than ours. Perhaps the cuts are generally simpler, require less precision, the woods softer and not as dry. Granted, these could be factors, although in the case described they are not, and if anything, hardwoods, primarily mahogany, are the indigenous varieties.

However, these are all speculations, no better than your own. As ergonomists, however, consider how we can adapt the tool to the Haitian culture, with the least disruption and at minimal cost, bearing in mind that no manufacturer is going to re-tool to meet the requirements of a few hundred Haitians. Anything we suggest must be within the capacity of the Haitians themselves, with their own limited resources.

Improvements might include anything from reshaping the blade, to reorientation of the teeth, to redesign of the handle. In the light of the constraints, however, repositioning and redesign of the handle may be the only practical solution. Trying to change the blade would be too costly and require that the old saw be abandoned altogether. Fashioning a new wooden handle or an attachment, however, would be feasible, inexpensive, and relatively simple. After all, these are woodworkers.

An attachment for the handle could be considered to provide a more sizeable and better grip. This would accommodate the application of force and not interfere with the cutting task. The saw would retain its original handle, or some modified version of it to be used, where necessary, in the conventional manner. Ideally, the object would be detachable. Extension of the handle is the essential characteristic being sought, so the attachment could be a simple object, a cutaway, hollow shaft or sleeve fitting over the existing handle and/or bolted to it, but all run the risk of making the task clumsier.

If one recognizes that the biggest problem with the unconventional grip is the limited finger space (see Fig. XI-11), a simple solution, though perhaps far from ideal, might be to use the existing handle as a basic pattern, but making the handle opening the same width in both dimensions and in effect enlarging the finger space. This would accommodate either mode of use and would be representative of something already familiar to the Haitian carpenter. Furthermore, retrofitting would be a nominal task. Simpler still, perhaps a small piece of the existing handle should be cut out to provide passage for the fingers, thus limiting the amount of interference they experience.

As an alternative, a machete-type handle might be considered with its gently curving, pistol grip similar in shape to the turn of the century musket handle or handgun. It would have several advantages. Firstly, the design is very familiar to most Haitian workers. A machete is one of the most common tools. Secondly, it would allow use of a strong power grip. Thirdly, the application of force would be more directly in line with the cutting edge and not at an angle as is found when using an conventional grip on the existing handle. Fourthly, because of the pistol shape, the saw could be used in the conventional fashion as we know it. Finally, and not the least important, handles of this type are readily available in the third world.

Case XII

THE SULLEN SECRETARIES

Mr. Matson can't keep a secretary for more than a few months. It's not that he's a poor boss. In fact, his secretaries have all thought he's very good to work for—firm, fair, considerate and not capriciously demanding—although his secretary is required to put in a good solid seven to eight hours' work in each working day, and generally several hours of overtime in the course of a week.

The office of the secretary is pleasant, warmly decorated and air conditioned, with a carpet, bright walls, two attractive paintings, and good quality furniture. The desk is the kind of furniture that one could have at home—walnut, with a shiny top, 32″ high by 56″ wide by 32″ deep, two pedestals and a kneehole. It has a credenza on the right side at the same height. One wall of the office, opposite the door to the boss's office, has a window approximately 5′ high by 3′ wide. The secretary sits with her back to the window. The window gives a good strong light to her desk, strong enough that she can see its reflection in the display of her computer terminal. In summer, indeed, she needs to close the curtains to cut down the glare, an action which in turn causes a nice reflection of the curtains to appear on her display. Mounted on the desk, in addition to a walnut in/out tray, telephone, address file and other secretarial appurtenances, is a personal computer terminal and keyboard with a polished black finish. The terminal display unit is off to the right of the computer, half on the desk and half on the credenza, but angled a little towards the secretary. The printer for the terminal is on the credenza, but she can reach it by swivelling the stool and using her feet to creep the stool over.

The stool is a fairly standard office stool on four legs. It is made of metal and has a contoured wooden seat, with a slight backwards tilt. The seat is mounted on a central telescopic pedestal held in position by a wheel knob, tightening of which requires a good strong hand. It can be adjusted from a low of 15″ at the front to a high of 18″, although it is normally kept in the low position. The backrest can be moved backwards or forwards as required and fixed by a wheel knob. The backrest has a 2″

149

curvature and pivots about 20 degrees in the vertical plane. It too can be adjusted for height over a range of 6″ and fixed by a wheel knob.

Attractive filing cabinets and a work table are located against a non-window wall, while doors to the boss's office and to a storage and cloak closet are on the wall opposite the secretary's position.

The room lighting is by way of the window and two unshielded overhead fluorescent tube fixtures which hang down from the ceiling. The effect is to produce an ambient illumination level of about 100 lux, although the lighting at the window desk in direct sunlight is about 750 lux.

THE PROBLEM

As noted earlier, the problem is certainly not with Mr. Matson himself, nor does it derive from the ambience of the surroundings, which indeed are very pleasant. The problem, as Mr. Matson sees it, is one of rapid turnover. None of his secretaries want the job on a permanent basis. Indeed, no matter how good they appeared to be when they were first hired, their performance would begin to fall off after a few months on the job. Daily output would become less; there would be less willingness to do overtime, even at a higher pay rate; complaints of symptoms such as fatigue, backache, headache, neck ache, shoulder ache would emerge; eyes would begin to smart after an hour or so at work, with more difficulty focussing, and so on. Male or female (and he tried both), it made no difference. Some of his secretaries in the past, indeed, particularly any who were pregnant, used to wonder aloud, and even suggest to Mr. Matson, that their problems might be caused by radiation from the VDT (video display terminal); while others considered that in spite of the pleasant surroundings they just couldn't put up with the physical strain. One way or another, each of them would leave to find some other work.

Mr. Matson, who is a lawyer specializing in divorce settlements, also has a VDT which he uses sporadically for an hour or so each day. From his own experience he knows that VDT work is not all that demanding. He may feel overworked occasionally, but he doesn't blame his VDT. Nevertheless, after losing five secretaries in the course of two years he thinks he'd better check out their work stations. He calls in an ergonomist to assist him.

ASSIGNMENT

As a consulting ergonomist you are required to present a report to Mr. Matson outlining from an ergonomic viewpoint the needs of an ideal VDT work station, and the faults and limitations existing in his system that might be responsible for the problems of his secretaries. Particular attention should be paid to the role of VDT radiation, the suitability of office furniture and its placement, the location of VDT equipment, the effects of illumination and glare, and the fact that Mr. Matson's experience is in contrast with that of his secretaries. Appropriate recommendations should be made.

THE SULLEN SECRETARIES SOLUTION

What we are dealing with here is a fatigue syndrome which is not uncommon among full-time users of VDT equipment and furniture that is not ergonomically suitable. The fatigue that is occurring is no doubt aggravated still further by excessive glare and inadequate illumination, while, of course, the hours of work, although not grossly excessive, might be considered demanding if Mr. Madison expects as much work out of his secretaries as he does of himself. Not all persons share the same expectations.

In this connection, it might be noted that Mr. Matson's experience and VDT usage is significantly different from that of his secretaries. As an executive, rather than a clerical worker, his use of the VDT is relatively minor and is largely unaffected by any work station problems. In addition, his use of the system is under his own control and oriented towards achieving his own objectives, while that of the secretaries is full time, not under their control, and indeed is an end in itself. Thus, any dissatisfaction they may experience tends to be directed towards the system, while any that Mr. Matson might feel would be directed not towards the system but to the nature of the work itself.

VDT Radiation

The question of VDT radiation is one that has concerned VDT operators for over twenty years. During that period well-publicized clusters of conditions such as spontaneous abortion and birth of deformed babies have occasionally occurred among VDT workers. Statistically, however, it has been shown that these clusters occur just as readily by simple chance. There is no doubt that a VDT unit generates certain types of radiant energy, and also there is no doubt that sufficient exposure to x-radiation can cause the kind of damage described above. A cathode ray tube (CRT) mechanism, which is the operating basis of a VDT display, *can* produce damaging x-radiation from the high voltage electron gun

152

which paints the picture. The CRT used in a VDT, however, or for that matter in a television set, is not the same as those used for medical imaging, industrial and other purposes. The latter operate at a voltage much higher than that found in a VDT. Consequently, there is no reason to consider that x-radiation from VDTs is a source of hazard.

On the other hand, a VDT does generate other forms of radiation. Infrared and ultraviolet radiation derive from interaction of the electron beam with the phosphors on the inside of the glass of the CRT. But while each of these forms of radiation, for example, in excessive sun exposure or in welding without protection, can give rise to irritation of and damage to the skin and eyes, there is no evidence of any such effect on VDT operators.

Pulsed radiofrequency energy from the mechanisms that control the flow of dots that make the display can also be measured, but again there is no substantiated evidence that radio frequency energy can cause adverse effects in human tissue. Microwave energy, which can be harmful, just does not occur in VDTs.

There are three other sources of energy of interest in VDTs, namely, extremely low frequency radiation (ELF), and electric and magnetic fields. The effects of ELF are still under discussion, but there is no consensus about any adverse results. Static negative charge on the surface of the screen, however, can attract positive ions from the skin surface of the face, if sufficiently close, and may give rise to a harmless skin rash which readily disappears in a fairly short time.

It is safe to say that there is no evidence that exposure to the radiation from VDTs is harmful to an operator, pregnant or not. Some companies, for psychological or political reasons, allow workers in the late stages of pregnancy to discontinue their VDT work. If there were any validity to the alleged radiation hazard, however, it would of course be better if the work were discontinued during the first three months, since it would be during that time that any fetal damage would occur.

Furniture and Equipment

The secretary's furniture is ergonomically unsuitable for continued VDT work. The dimensions of the desk are inappropriate, and the shiny walnut surface contributes to glare. Ideally, the VDT worker should be seated with the legs approximately at right angles to the thighs, with the forearms horizontal or sloping slightly downward. Normally this is achieved by fixing the desk height and adjusting the height of the seat accordingly. These circumstances are complicated, however, by having to allow for the keyboard. To account for both seated leg length and knee clearance (see Appendix 1), it therefore becomes necessary to provide a height of some 720–750 mm (28.5–29.5 in) to the centerline of the keyboard, of which 650–690 mm (25.5–27 in) should be free legroom. Since the desk itself is rarely less than 20–30 mm (3/4–1 in) in thickness and since the keyboard is rarely less than 35 mm (1¼ in) at its thickest dimension, it also becomes necessary to ensure that the desk is adjustable at two or more levels, one level on which to mount a keyboard, one for documentation and terminal, and perhaps still another for storage. It must also be ensured that all levels are simply adjustable, without tools or the need to use the services of some maintenance person, and that they are adjusted to meet the needs of the user when they are used.

Of at least as great significance is the stool or chair, which must be adjustable to allow the operator to work with the arms in the previously noted ideal position. It should have a rolled front so that the front edge does not cut into the soft tissues of the thigh and reduce the blood and nerve supply to the lower leg. A contoured wooden format such as is described here is undesirable. A seat should not be contoured to the form of the buttocks since an improper fit could give rise to undesirable compression of soft tissues just like a sharp front edge. It should have a cushioned and upholstered finish, rough textured and flexible to avoid slippage, and it should not have pressure points such as seams, buttons, or pleats. Recommended dimensions include a seat height of 380–500 mm (15–20 in), a seat width of 400 mm (15½–16 in), a seat back height 400 mm (15¾ in) above the height of the seat cushion, with a back angle of 5–10 degrees, a pivoting curved seat back with a width of 300–450 mm (12–17½ in), detachable seat arms 230–280 mm (9–11 in) above the seat cushion and 300 mm (12 in) in length. Although it is often considered by some that armrests are an impediment to effective keyboard work, this is not so. Armrests should be provided on the seat. They should be padded and should not cut into the arm or create pinch points. The base of the seat should be stable, preferably with five feet rather than four, and with a base diameter of 400–450 mm (16–18 in).

To maintain the legs in a relatively comfortable and ideal posture it may be necessary to provide a footstool. Ideally, the footstool should be separate from the chair and the desk, with a height adjustable to approximately 50–75 mm (2–3 in) at the upper end with an inclination angle of 10–15 degrees from the horizontal. It should have a nonslip undersurface.

The fact that the existing furniture does not meet these specifications, and that in particular the desk is too high with a surface that does not readily accommodate the keyboard, requires the operator to work in an awkward posture with the arms upraised to position the hands on the keyboard, and with the legs pressured by the edge of the seat. This posture in turn may produce stress on the back and shoulder muscles, with resulting discomfort, aching, and pain in the back, shoulders and arms, sometimes with swelling of the ankles, along with generalized, and eventually unacceptable, fatigue.

The computer equipment also bears consideration. No doubt it is functionally very effective. That is not the consideration. The polished black finish, however, contributes to the glare. Equipment which has a matte black or, even better, a matte grey non-reflecting surface is less reflective. The location on the desk is also unsatisfactory. Since the display is located partially on the credenza, the operator has to turn her head continually as she scans her copywork, her keyboard, and the display. These actions, of course, contribute markedly to her neck ache and headache. Ideally, the range of view of the display should lie in the midline of sight, some 32–40 degrees below the horizontal, with an optimum centerline 20 degrees below the horizontal. Unfortunately, these requirements are rarely achieved. The situation here, however, would be greatly improved by placing the display immediately in front of the operator and locating the terminal where the display is currently found.

Illumination and Glare

Illumination and glare are major problems here. Of these, glare is probably the more serious, and in the course of seven to eight hours work plus overtime it must contribute significantly to the visual problems encountered by the secretaries. Glare can be direct or reflected, direct occurring when there is a bright source directly in the visual field, and reflected when the bright light is reflected from surfaces to the eyes. The glare here, of course, is derived largely from reflected window light and to some extent from the overhead fixtures. The reflective surfaces are the polished desk, papers, and so on, and the equipment itself, particularly the display screen. Screening the window with curtains may reduce the source of the glare but, as noted in the text, produces a patterned reflection on the screen which is no less disturbing. Without converting entirely to artificial light it is not feasible to screen the window completely. Loss of the window is neither practicable nor desirable. Psychologically, a window is a desirable asset in an office.

A feasible solution to the glare problem lies then in either or both of two approaches. Firstly, whenever practicable the desk and its appurtenances should be replaced by an ergonomically designed, computer compatible work station, with non-reflecting surfaces. As noted already, the computer equipment should also be changed, and any reflecting materials on the desk should be removed. Secondly, and of even more practical significance, the location of the desk should be moved to a position at right angles to the window, such that in this case the secretary now has the window on her left side. Reflectance will be much less, and in particular there will be no window reflectance on the display.

The general illumination also is inadequate and improperly distributed. There is still some controversy over the ideal level of general illumination in offices, but most employees in general offices prefer levels between 400 and 850 lux. Levels above 1000 lux tend to increase the potential for glare. For VDT offices, however, where the operator is watching a somewhat dimly lit display, 400 lux is too high and creates too great a contrast. In the situation described here, where the walls are bright, a level of 250–300 lux from window and luminaires would probably be adequate, with additional local lighting at the desk if needed, provided that care is taken to avoid glare on the display screen and that the brightness contrast of 1:10 between the center of the display and the periphery of the center field (desk, keyboard, documents, and so on) is not exceeded. The two overhead lighting fixtures should be replaced with recessed and shielded luminaires, adequate to meet the illumination requirements and set at right angles to the secretary's line of sight to minimize direct glare.

Work Load

VDT work is sedentary, and while it is true that most daily workers even at heavy jobs work seven to eight hours a day with only standard coffee and lunch breaks, it should be recognized that the effort required in VDT work is intellectually concentrated and emotionally demanding. NIOSH, the National Institute for Occupational Safety and Health in the U.S., recommends that where the use of a VDT is intensive there should be additional breaks of fifteen minutes per hour. The work here is probably not that intensive, but consideration should be given to providing special breaks of five to ten minutes per hour in addition to the usual lunch breaks.

RECOMMENDATIONS

It is not practicable to make wholesale changes in the office environment virtually overnight, but as the time becomes feasible the following actions are suggested in the light of the foregoing discussion:

1. Replace the existing desk and credenza with an ergonomically designed, computer-compatible, non-reflecting work station.
2. Replace the existing stool with a chair designed for computer use.
3. Provide an adjustable footstool.
4. Relocate the computer work station at right angles to the window to minimize reflections.
5. Remove to the extent feasible all shiny surfaces from the immediate visual field.
6. When replacing existing computer equipment, purchase equipment finished in a matte grey surface.
7. Relocate the terminal display directly in front of the secretary. Mount the printer on top of the computer terminal in a position readily accessible to the secretary.
8. Reorganize work surfaces around the secretary to provide a close work area containing units in frequent use such as keyboard, display and immediate documents; a convenient area for units in occasional use such as telephone and secondary documents; and a maximum reach area for units in infrequent use, such as reference documents, printer, computer, and so on.
9. Replace overhead hanging light fixtures with recessed shielded luminaries, increasing the number if necessary to meet the illumination requirements.
10. Provide educational material and counselling to acquaint the secretary with the significance of VDT radiation.
11. When work load is heavy, allow short recess every hour, along with standard lunch and coffee breaks.

APPENDICES

Appendix 1

ANTHROPOMETRY

The term anthropometry derives from two Greek words, *anthropos,* meaning man, and *metros,* meaning measurement. In other words, anthropometry is concerned with the measurement of human dimensions. Many hundreds of these dimensions are possible, everything from the common measurement of stature, or height, to the size of a human fingernail, but of these, a hundred or more have been defined as being useful for various purposes, such as for the design of seats, the working height of benches, the size of tool handles, the accessibility of entrances and exits, the placement of displays and controls, the ability to lift and carry, the size of clothing, and so on. Some of these measures are quite esoteric and are of use for special purposes only, but some selected measures are appended in the tables below.

In using anthropometric measures there are several things to bear in mind. One of these is the source of the measures. All anthropometric tables present values which are statistical in nature. In other words they are derived as averages of multiple samples, sometimes from hundreds, sometimes thousands of subjects. The larger the sample, the more representative it is or in statistical terms the greater is the accuracy and confidence in the measured value. It is difficult to get large enough samples of human subjects who are prepared to stand still long enough to be measured in perhaps a hundred different dimensions. Consequently, most statistical samples are derived from young, healthy, military populations which are certainly not representative of the total population. The resulting values have to be applied with care but are useful for most purposes. However, there are relatively few data available for small children, for various ethnic groups, for the elderly, the disabled, the infirm, and for different social classes. Secondly, the subjects in these samples are measured under standard conditions, for example, standing erect in minimal clothing, looking straight ahead with shoulders relaxed and arms hanging loosely, or seated pulled up to full height, conditions which are seldom representative of working postures in an operational environment. Consequently, both clothing and a slumping posture can significantly change a measure.

Thirdly, consider the various meanings of the term *average.* In statistics, the average value has a specific definition, whereas in everyday language it may mean more than one thing. In everyday language an average can be taken to refer to a mean, a median, or a mode, but in statistics these are three very different concepts. A *mean* is derived as the sum of all the individual measurements divided by the number of measurements. The mean may not correspond exactly with any one of the measured values. For example, it is commonly stated that the average family nowadays has 1.8 children. This is not a measured, but a derived value taking into account, not only the number of children per family, but also the number of families. This is an example of the most common meaning for the term *average* and is consistent with the statistical definition of the term. A *median* divides the measurements into two equally sized groups, separating the lower values from the higher values, so that there are as many measurements above the median as there are below. The median represents an actual measurement value. For example, the middle finger represents the median finger position on the hand, with the thumb and index finger on one side, the ring finger and pinkie on the other side. The *mode* is the most frequently occurring value in the set of measurements. For example, in a popularity contest the most highly preferred color, style, model, represents the modal value.

In designing for human use the average or *mean* value of a human dimension often is not the best, nor the only choice and can be very misleading or restrictive. For example, if a seat in an aircraft were designed based on the average width at the hips, then half the population could not sit in the seat without discomfort, since by definition half the people would have hips wider than the mean value, and only half would have hips narrow enough to fit into the seat.

As a result, in designing for human performance, attention is often paid to the use of *critical* dimensions based on still another statistical concept, the *percentile* (%ile). A percentile value divides the measurements into groups of variable size, with 100 percent representing the uppermost limit of all of the measurements, and 50 percent representing the median or 50th percentile. Likewise, any number of values between 0 and 100 may be used to subdivide the measurements and to indicate the percentage of the measurements/population that is equal to or below a certain critical or design value. Thus a 95th %ile would encompass all values equal to or less than 95% of the measurements, and a 5th %ile would encompass all values equal to or less than 5% of the same. Going back to the previous example, to design a seat that would accommodate most of the population, a 95th %ile value would be chosen for hip width. If the objective was to keep something low enough so that most persons could reach it, you would design to a 5th %ile value.

The tables below show some selected body dimensions, but the data are not genuine. The measurements in these tables have been generated to be approximately representative of mixed European, mixed U.S. and mixed Asian populations. They have been generated solely for the purpose of this exercise, and it is emphasized that the data listed here should not be used for any purposes other than completing some of the exercises in this book. For simplicity, much important information is not included, such as the statistical calculation of the standard deviation, which shows the amount of variation in that sample, nor how and where the data were derived.

Presented in the tables are data representative of an American population, as well as data representative of European and Asian populations. Remember, however, that there is great diversity within populations as well as between populations, such that, for example, when averaging over a mixed population the data for American

Hispanics may not be the same as for American Blacks, although for our purposes the numerical values given are adequate. The tables show estimates of dimensions for males and females in the 5th, 50th, and 95th percentile categories. You will recognize that the 50th percentile is the same as the median. All values are in inches. Some corrections for special circumstance can be made as follows:

Clothing (including shoes):

Standing height:	+1.00 in
Sitting height:	+0.25 in
Breadth:	+0.33 in
Foot length:	+1.25 in

Postural slump:

Standing:	−0.75 in
Sitting:	−1.75 in

Other corrections:

Additional height on tiptoe:	3.00 in
Reduced height by squatting:	6.00 in
Extended reach, bending from waist:	7.25 in
Extended reach, bending from hips:	14.0 in

As a point of interest, the actual anthropometric differences between the industrial nations of the USA, Germany, France and Great Britain are said to be so slight that they can be neglected. Grandjean[1] gives the following measures for adult males to illustrate. In these groups the population means for selected dimensions vary as follows:

1) Body length: 170–173 cm
2) Back to front of knee: 59–60 cm
3) Top of knee to floor: 54–55 cm
4) Elbow to floor: 105–107 cm

1. Grandjean, Etienne: *Ergonomics in Computerized Offices.* London, New York and Philadelphia, Taylor and Francis, 1987, p. 101.

Appendix 2

ANTHROPOMETRIC ESTIMATES FOR U.S. ADULTS, MIXED POPULATION (IN); MIXED EUROPEAN ADULT POPULATION (IN); AND MIXED ASIAN ADULT POPULATION (IN)

Table A1-1
ANTHROPOMETRIC ESTIMATES FOR
U.S. ADULTS, MIXED POPULATION (in)

	(Men (%ile)			*Women (%ile)*		
	5th	50th	95th	5th	50th	95th
Dimension						
1. Stature	64.5	69.0	73.5	59.5	63.5	68.0
2. Sitting height	33.5	36.0	38.5	31.5	34.0	36.0
3. Vertical grip reach						
standing	77.0	82.0	87.0	71.0	75.5	80.5
sitting	45.5	49.5	53.5	42.5	47.5	49.0
4. Forward grip reach — *standing*						
center	29.0	31.0	33.5	26.0	28.0	30.0

Table A1-2
ANTHROPOMETRIC ESTIMATES FOR
MIXED EUROPEAN ADULT POPULATION (in)

	(Men (%ile)			*Women (%ile)*		
	5th	50th	95th	5th	50th	95th
Dimension						
1. Stature	64.0	68.5	73.0	59.0	63.5	68.0
2. Sitting height	33.0	35.5	38.0	31.0	33.5	36.0
3. Vertical grip reach						
standing	75.5	81.0	86.0	70.5	74.5	79.5
sitting	45.0	49.0	52.5	41.5	45.0	48.5
4. Forward grip reach — *standing*						
center	28.5	30.5	33.0	25.5	27.5	29.5

*Summated data prepared by authors.

Table A1-3
ANTHROPOMETRIC ESTIMATES FOR
MIXED ASIAN ADULT POPULATION (in)

	Men (%ile)			Women (%ile)		
	5th	50th	95th	5th	50th	95th
Dimensions						
1. Stature	61.5	65.0	69.0	57.0	60.0	63.5
2. Sitting height	32.5	35.0	37.5	30.5	33.0	35.0
3. Vertical grip reach						
standing	71.0	76.5	81.5	67.5	72.0	76.5
sitting	43.5	46.5	50.0	40.5	43.0	45.5
4. Forward grip reach — *standing*						
center	25.0	27.0	30.0	22.5	24.5	26.5

Appendix 3

NIOSH LIFTING GUIDELINES
NATIONAL INSTITUTE FOR
OCCUPATIONAL HEALTH AND SAFETY

In considering lifting tasks two considerations must be borne in mind, namely, the acute effects of over stressing the back and the cumulative demands on the back and other joints of the body from repeated lifting day after day for many months or years. Lifting limit guidelines need to recognize both.

After studying the various approaches that have been made towards defining lifting standards, NIOSH developed a model for the purpose. The NIOSH method defines two lifting limits, namely, the Action Limit and the Maximum Permissible Limit, which are described below. The limits presented do not, however, apply to all kinds of lifts. It is assumed in the model that the lift is a smooth two-handed symmetrical lift directly in front of the body, with no twisting during lifting. The object is assumed to be no wider than 75 cm (30 in), and the lifting posture is assumed to be unrestricted with good coupling between hands and object.

Action Limit (AL)

The Action Limit, as the term implies, represents a threshold for lifting beyond which action is recommended to alleviate the physical demands of manual handling. The limit is unique to the task and determined by certain physiological capacities to provide strength, stamina, tolerance, and endurance. An action may constitute any number of administrative procedures and/or engineering controls which reduce the physiological burdens associated with the lifting task. Lifting conditions which do not cross the threshold are considered to be safe for the majority of workers.

The Action Limit is intended to control the incidence of back injury and to define reasonable expectations for energy output. It is believed, therefore, that tasks which adhere to the Action Limit:

a) permit only a moderate increase, if any, in musculoskeletal problems in a population exposed to these lifting conditions.

b) ensure that compression on the spine will not exceed 350 kg (770 lb) of force, a level which can be tolerated by most young workers without incident.

c) ensure that the metabolic rate of workers in these conditions will not exceed 3.5 kilocalories per minute, a level which has been shown to be within acceptable levels of energy expenditure, and

d) represent tolerable load handling for over 99% of males and 75% of females.

Maximum Permissible Limit (MPL)

The Maximum Permissible Limit as the term implies represents an upper limit which should not be exceeded. It is a multiple of the Action Limit, and hence is also task specific. Unlike the AL, the MPL does not represent a working limit, but a cutoff value, a ceiling value. The MPL is based on recognition of the following facts, that:

a) the incidence of musculoskeletal injury tends to increase significantly among populations where work exceeds the MPL value.

b) pressure forces on the spine are not tolerable in most workers at lifting levels above the MPL.

c) metabolic rates among most persons working above the MPL will exceed 5.0 kilocalories, a level of energy expenditure that is not acceptable for continuous activity, and

d) only 25% of males and less than 1% of females are able to perform work above the MPL.

According to the NIOSH guidelines, lifting demands above the MPL are unacceptable for working conditions. Engineering intervention is required in order to prevent injury.

Lifts may be defined as acceptable if the Action Limit is not exceeded, unacceptable if the MPL is exceeded and acceptable with modifications for tasks which fall in between the two limits.

The NIOSH Formula

The NIOSH guidelines defines three broad categories of lifting, namely:

Infrequent lifting: Lifting that is performed either occasionally, or continuously at a rate of less than one lift every three minutes,

Occasional high frequency lifting: lifting once or more often every three minutes continuously for a period of up to one hour,

Continuous high frequency lifting: lifting once or more often every three minutes continuously for eight hours.

The limitation on infrequent lifting is largely determined by musculoskeletal strength, the high stress loading on the back being the primary limitation. Occasional high frequency lifting may be limited in addition by human endurance and muscle fatigue. For continuous high frequency lifting there is an additional limitation imposed by cardiovascular and metabolic factors.

The *Action Limit* is defined in the following terms:

$$AL \text{ (lb)} = 90(6/H)(1.0 - 0.01|V - 30|)(0.7 + 3/D)(1 - FF_{max})$$

$$AL \text{ (kg)} = 40(15/H)(1.0 - 0.004|V - 75|)(0.7 + 7.5/D)(1 - F/F_{max})$$

where

H = horizontal location (in/cm) of the load at origin of lift, forward of the midpoint between the ankles

V = vertical location (in/cm) of object at origin of lift measured from the floor

D = vertical travel distance (in/cm) between the origin and destination of lift, and

F = average frequency of lifting

The following limitations apply to these variables:

a) H is assumed to lie between 15 cm (6 in) and 80 cm (32 in) since objects in general cannot be closer to the focus of spinal loading because of interference from the human body, and cannot be further away than 32 inches without an intolerable reach.

b) V is assumed to lie between 0 cm and 175 cm (70 in), namely, the vertical reach limits of most persons.

c) D is assumed to lie between 25 cm (10 in) and 200-V cm (80-V in). For lifts which involve small displacements of less than 25 cm, the minimum value is assigned.

d) F is assumed to be between 0.2 (1 lift every 5 minutes) and F_{max}. For lifts which are performed less than once every 5 minutes, F is set at zero.

e) F_{max} for periods of 1 hr has a value of 18 or 15, where V is greater or less than 30 in (75 cm) respectively, that is, for the stooped or standing postures. F_{max} for an eight-hour workday is 15 or 12, where V is greater or less than 30 in (75 cm), respectively.

In the formula 90 lb or 40 kg represent the Action Limits under ideal conditions. The various factors discount the limit. If the H factor, that is (15/H), is 15 cm, then obviously no modification is required. Similarly, when the V factor, the absolute value of V-75, is 75 cm, again no modification occurs. As D varies from a minimum of 25 cm to a maximum of 200 cm, the D factor ranges from 1 to 0.74, as already noted.

An illustration demonstrating these various factors as they pertain to the 1981 NIOSH guidelines is shown in Figure A2-1. NIOSH has not officially released any revisions to guidelines described above, although there is consideration being given to ways of improving the work practice guidelines. The amended formula may introduce additional factors to take into account the asymmetric lifting postures which are not uncommon and differences in the effectiveness of the grip. The influence of the **H, V** and **D** factors may change slightly under the proposed guidelines after being reevaluated. In general, the proposed limits would be more stringent.

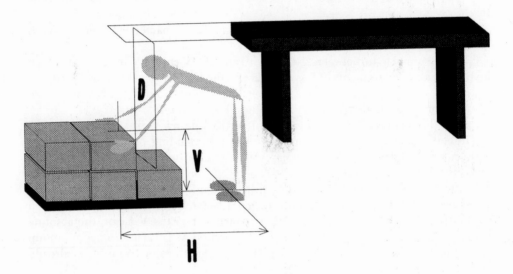

Figure A2-1.

Appendix 4

SNOOK AND CIRIELLO LIFTING GUIDELINES

Over the past twenty years the above authors have studied a variety of manual handling capabilities, including the ability of industrial workers to lift, carry and lower weights. They have performed laboratory simulations of industrial tasks with the subjects handling industrial tote boxes. Their tests incorporated various physiological and anthropometric measurements and attempted to make the experimental tasks as realistic as possible. Tests were conducted using industrial workers from the local community.

The results are based exclusively on one method, namely, the psychophysical approach, in which the subject is given control of either the amount of weight or the amount of force applied. The other variables, such as frequency, size of the load, the travel distance, and so on, are controlled by the experimenter. Subjects monitor their own feelings of exertion and fatigue and adjust the weight or force accordingly. In contrast, the NIOSH studies integrate several different approaches including data from Snook and colleagues.

The nomenclature between the Snook and Ciriello data and the NIOSH studies varies, but the factors that describe the lifts and load handling are to a certain extent the same. The variable Snook and Ciriello identify as *box width* has an equivalency in the NIOSH formula, namely, the **H** factor. Their *distance* variable represents the amount of travel in transferring the load from the point of origin to the destination, as it does in the NIOSH equation. But some fundamental differences exist. Snook and Ciriello use descriptive categories based on anatomical reference points to identify the type of lift, rather than an independent variable to describe the point of origin. Thus, whereas the NIOSH formula has a **V** factor which defines the point of origin with reference to the floor, lifts according to the Snook and Ciriello scheme fall into one of three categories, as lifting between the floor and knuckle height,[1] between knuckle height and the shoulders,[2] and lifting above the shoulders.[3]

Snook and Ciriello present their data in tabulated form, rather than a formula, making direct interpretations possible if manual handling tasks fall within the ranges they describe. In each of the above mentioned categories they provide data

---

1. Knuckle height is the distance from the floor to the knuckles with the hands held closely alongside the body while standing erect. Lifts in this category are low lifts which can only be performed by stooping over and/or crouching.

2. Lifts in this category may be performed in a standing posture, with minimal bending.

3. Lifts above the shoulders and head require upper body strength and are fundamentally different from the low lifts which use muscles in the back and abdomen.

171

on three lifting *distances* ranging from short 25 cm (10 in) lifts to longer 76 cm (30 in) lifts performed at frequencies ranging from one lift every 5 seconds to one lift per eight-hour working shift. Lifts are assumed to take place within the middle of the lifting range, the greater distances spanning a larger part of the lifting range. Where lifts being evaluated do not correspond directly with the information provided, some further interpolations are possible. Data are presented for three different load (horizontal reach) dimensions defined by *box widths* of 34, 49 and 75 cm (14, 20, and 30 in).

Tables showing the maximum acceptable weight of lifting for both males and females are reproduced* for your convenience. Unlike the NIOSH limits which represent only the values likely to be acceptable to most industrial workers, Snook and Ciriello further classify the lifting abilities of the industrial population. Separate guidelines are presented for the group containing 90% of the industrial workers, 75%, 50% and 10%, respectively, the former representing tasks that are likely to be acceptable to most workers, the latter representing work that is likely to be acceptable to only a few of the stronger, more fit workers. There is no direct correspondence to the NIOSH *Action Limit* which integrates the data for males and females. The *Action Limit* represents lifts that are believed to be acceptable for 99% of male workers and 75% of female workers.

NIOSH guidelines do not cover tasks other than lifting, but a considerable amount of manual handling involves other activities. Tables showing the maximum acceptable weights for lowering and carrying are also reproduced from Snook and Ciriello to assist the reader in evaluating such tasks. Other helpful information on task involving pushing and pulling of loads can be found in Snook and Ciriello.

---

*Reproduced with the kind permission of the authors and their publisher.

Snook SH and VM Ciriello. The design of manual handling tasks: revised tables of maximum acceptable weights and forces. *Ergonomics*, V34, 1197–1213, 1991.

Table A3-1: MAXIMUM ACCEPTABLE WEIGHT OF LIFT FOR MALES (kg)

Width‡	Distance§	Percent¶	Floor level to knuckle height — One lift every								Knuckle height to shoulder height — One lift every								Shoulder height to arm reach — One lift every							
			5 s	9 s	14 s	1 min	2 min	5 min	30 min	8 h	5 s	9 s	14 s	1 min	2 min	5 min	30 min	8 h	5 s	9 s	14 s	1 min	2 min	5 min	30 min	8 h
75	76	90	6	7	9	11	13	14	14	17	8	10	12	13	14	14	16	17	6	8	9	10	10	11	12	13
		75	9	11	13	16	19	20	21	24	10	14	16	18	18	19	21	23	8	10	12	14	14	14	16	17
		50	12	15	17	22	25	27	28	32	13	17	20	23	23	24	26	29	10	13	15	17	17	18	20	22
		25	15	18	21	28	31	34	35	41	16	21	24	27	27	28	32	35	11	16	18	21	21	22	24	27
		10	18	22	25	33	37	40	41	48	19	24	28	31	32	33	37	40	14	18	21	24	24	25	28	31
	51	90	6	8	9	12	13	15	15	17	8	11	13	15	15	15	18	19	6	8	9	12	12	12	14	15
		75	9	11	13	17	19	21	22	25	11	15	17	20	20	21	23	25	8	11	12	15	15	16	18	20
		50	13	15	18	23	26	28	29	34	14	19	22	25	25	26	29	32	10	14	16	19	20	20	23	25
		25	16	19	22	29	33	35	36	42	17	23	26	30	31	32	36	39	13	17	19	23	24	25	27	30
		10	19	22	26	34	35	42	43	50	20	26	30	35	36	37	41	45	15	19	22	27	27	29	32	35
	25	90	8	9	11	13	15	16	17	20	10	13	15	18	18	18	21	23	7	10	11	14	14	14	16	18
		75	11	13	15	19	22	24	24	28	13	17	20	23	24	24	27	30	9	13	15	18	18	19	21	23
		50	15	18	21	26	29	32	33	38	17	22	25	30	30	31	35	38	12	16	19	23	23	24	27	29
		25	19	22	26	33	37	40	41	48	20	27	31	36	36	38	42	46	15	20	22	28	28	29	32	35
		10	22	26	31	38	44	47	49	57	23	31	35	42	42	44	49	53	17	23	26	32	32	34	38	41
49	76	90	7	8	10	13	15	16	17	20	8	10	12	13	14	14	16	17	7	9	10	12	12	13	14	16
		75	10	12	14	19	22	24	24	28	11	14	16	18	18	19	21	23	9	11	13	16	16	17	19	21
		50	14	16	19	26	29	32	33	38	13	17	21	22	23	24	26	29	11	15	17	20	20	21	24	26
		25	17	20	24	33	37	40	41	48	16	21	24	27	27	28	32	35	13	18	20	25	25	26	29	31
		10	20	24	28	38	43	47	48	57	19	24	28	31	32	33	37	40	15	21	23	29	29	30	33	36
	51	90	7	9	10	14	16	17	18	20	8	11	13	15	15	16	18	19	7	9	11	14	14	14	16	18
		75	10	13	15	20	23	25	25	30	11	15	17	20	20	21	23	25	9	12	14	18	18	18	21	23
		50	14	17	20	27	30	33	34	40	14	19	22	25	25	26	29	32	11	15	18	23	23	24	26	29
		25	18	21	25	34	43	42	43	50	17	23	26	30	31	32	36	39	14	19	21	28	28	29	33	35
		10	21	25	29	40	49	49	50	59	20	26	30	35	36	37	41	45	16	22	25	32	33	34	38	41
	25	90	8	9	12	16	18	19	20	23	10	13	15	18	18	19	21	23	8	11	13	16	16	17	19	21
		75	12	15	17	23	26	28	29	33	13	17	20	23	24	25	27	30	11	14	17	21	21	22	25	27
		50	16	20	23	30	34	37	38	45	17	22	25	30	30	31	35	38	14	18	21	27	27	28	32	33
		25	20	24	29	38	43	47	48	56	20	27	30	36	36	38	42	45	16	22	25	33	33	34	38	42
		10	24	29	34	45	51	56	57	67	23	31	35	42	42	44	49	53	19	25	29	38	38	40	44	48
34	76	90	8	10	11	15	17	19	19	23	9	12	14	15	15	16	18	19	8	10	12	14	14	15	16	18
		75	12	14	17	22	28	28	28	33	12	16	18	20	20	21	23	25	10	14	16	18	18	19	22	24
		50	16	19	22	30	34	37	38	44	15	20	23	25	25	26	29	32	13	17	20	23	24	24	27	30
		25	20	24	28	37	42	47	47	55	18	24	27	31	31	32	36	39	16	21	24	28	29	30	33	36
		10	24	29	33	44	50	54	56	65	21	28	33	36	37	37	45	45	18	24	28	33	34	34	38	42
	51	90	9	10	12	16	18	20	20	24	9	12	14	17	17	18	20	22	8	11	13	16	16	17	18	20
		75	12	15	18	23	26	29	29	34	12	16	18	22	23	23	26	28	11	14	17	21	21	22	24	26
		50	17	20	24	31	35	38	39	46	16	20	24	29	29	30	33	35	14	18	21	26	27	28	31	34
		25	21	25	30	39	44	48	49	57	20	24	27	34	35	36	40	44	17	22	25	32	32	33	37	41
		10	25	30	35	46	52	57	58	68	24	28	32	40	40	42	46	51	19	26	29	37	37	39	43	47
	25	90	10	12	14	18	20	22	23	27	11	14	16	20	20	21	23	26	10	13	15	19	19	19	22	24
		75	15	18	21	26	32	32	33	38	14	18	21	26	27	28	31	34	13	17	20	24	24	26	29	31
		50	20	24	28	35	40	43	44	52	18	23	27	33	34	35	39	43	16	22	25	31	31	33	36	40
		25	26	30	35	44	50	54	55	65	21	28	32	40	41	42	47	52	20	26	30	37	38	39	44	46
		10	31	35	41	52	59	64	66	76	25	33	37	47	47	49	55	60	23	30	35	43	44	45	51	55

‡ Box width (the dimension away from the body) (cm).
§ Vertical distance of lift (cm).
¶ Percentage of industrial population.
Italicized values exceed 8 h physiological criteria (see text).

Table A3.2: MAXIMUM ACCEPTABLE WEIGHT OF LIFT FOR FEMALES (kg)

Width‡	Distance§	Percent¶	Floor level to knuckle height — One lift every								Knuckle height to shoulder height — One lift every								Shoulder height to arm reach — One lift every							
			5 s	9 s	14	1 min	2	5	30	8 h	5	9 s	14	1 min	2	5	30	8 h	5	9 s	14	1 min	2	5	30	8 h
75	76	90	5	6	7	7	8	8	9	12	5	6	7	9	9	9	10	12	4	5	5	6	7	7	7	8
		75	7	8	9	9	10	10	11	14	6	7	8	10	11	11	12	14	5	6	6	7	8	8	8	10
		50	8	10	11	11	12	12	13	17	7	8	9	11	12	12	13	16	6	7	7	8	9	9	10	11
		25	9	11	13	13	14	14	15	21	8	9	10	13	14	14	15	18	7	7	8	9	10	10	11	13
		10	11	13	14	14	16	16	17	23	9	10	11	14	15	15	17	20	7	8	9	10	11	11	12	14
	51	90	6	7	8	8	9	9	10	14	6	7	8	9	10	10	11	13	5	6	7	7	7	7	8	9
		75	9	9	10	10	11	11	13	17	7	8	9	11	12	12	13	15	6	7	8	8	9	9	9	11
		50	10	12	13	13	14	14	15	21	9	10	11	13	14	14	15	17	7	8	9	9	11	11	11	13
		25	11	14	15	15	16	16	17	24	10	12	13	15	16	16	17	20	8	8	10	10	12	12	13	14
		10	13	16	17	17	18	18	20	27	11	13	14	17	17	17	19	22	9	9	11	11	13	13	14	16
	25	90	6	8	8	9	9	9	10	14	6	7	8	10	11	11	12	14	5	6	7	8	8	8	9	10
		75	8	10	11	11	12	12	13	18	7	8	9	12	13	13	14	17	6	7	8	9	9	9	10	12
		50	9	11	13	13	14	14	16	21	8	10	11	14	15	15	16	19	7	8	9	10	11	11	12	14
		25	11	14	15	15	17	17	19	25	9	11	12	16	16	16	18	21	8	9	10	11	12	12	13	15
		10	13	16	17	17	19	19	21	29	11	12	14	18	17	17	19	24	9	10	11	13	14	14	15	17
49	76	90	5	6	7	8	8	8	9	13	5	6	7	9	9	9	10	12	4	5	5	7	7	7	8	9
		75	7	8	9	11	10	10	12	16	6	7	8	11	11	11	12	14	5	6	6	8	8	8	9	11
		50	9	10	11	13	13	13	14	19	7	8	9	13	12	12	13	16	6	7	7	9	9	9	11	12
		25	10	12	13	16	15	15	16	22	8	9	10	14	14	14	15	18	7	8	8	11	11	11	12	14
		10	11	14	15	18	17	17	19	26	9	10	11	16	15	15	17	20	7	8	9	11	11	11	13	15
	51	90	6	7	8	9	10	10	11	15	6	7	8	9	10	10	11	13	5	6	7	8	8	8	9	11
		75	9	9	11	11	12	12	14	18	7	8	9	11	12	12	13	15	6	7	8	9	9	9	10	13
		50	10	12	13	15	15	15	16	22	9	10	11	13	14	14	15	17	7	8	9	11	11	11	12	15
		25	11	14	16	16	17	17	20	26	10	11	12	15	16	16	17	20	8	9	10	12	12	12	13	17
		10	11	15	18	19	20	20	22	30	11	12	14	16	17	17	19	22	9	10	11	14	14	14	16	19
	25	90	6	8	8	9	9	10	11	15	7	7	8	10	10	10	11	13	5	6	7	8	9	9	10	11
		75	8	10	11	12	13	13	14	19	8	9	11	12	12	12	13	15	6	7	8	9	10	10	11	13
		50	10	11	13	15	15	15	17	23	9	11	11	14	14	14	16	17	7	8	9	11	12	12	13	15
		25	11	14	16	18	18	18	20	27	11	13	13	16	16	16	18	20	8	9	10	12	13	13	15	17
		10	13	16	17	19	21	21	23	31	13	14	14	18	17	17	19	22	9	10	11	14	15	15	16	19
34	76	90	7	8	9	11	11	12	13	18	7	8	9	9	10	10	11	13	8	7	7	8	9	9	10	11
		75	9	10	12	14	14	15	16	22	8	10	11	11	12	12	13	15	8	8	8	9	10	10	11	13
		50	11	12	14	16	17	18	20	27	10	11	11	13	14	14	16	17	10	10	10	11	12	12	13	15
		25	13	15	17	19	21	22	24	32	12	14	14	15	16	16	18	20	10	11	10	12	13	13	15	17
		10	14	18	19	22	24	25	28	36	13	16	17	18	19	19	21	24	11	12	11	14	15	15	16	19
	51	90	8	9	9	11	12	12	13	18	8	8	9	10	11	11	12	14	7	7	8	9	9	9	10	11
		75	9	11	12	14	15	15	16	22	9	10	11	12	13	13	14	16	8	8	9	10	11	11	12	13
		50	12	13	14	17	19	19	21	27	10	12	13	14	16	16	18	21	10	10	11	11	12	12	14	15
		25	13	14	17	19	22	24	24	32	12	14	14	16	18	18	19	24	11	11	12	13	13	13	15	18
		10	14	17	19	22	24	25	27	36	13	15	16	18	19	19	21	27	11	12	13	14	15	15	16	19
	25	90	8	10	11	11	12	12	14	19	8	10	10	12	13	13	14	16	7	7	8	9	10	10	11	12
		75	10	12	13	14	15	15	16	23	9	12	12	13	14	14	16	18	8	8	9	10	12	12	12	14
		50	12	15	16	17	19	19	21	28	10	13	13	16	17	17	19	21	9	10	11	12	13	13	14	17
		25	14	17	19	22	24	24	24	33	12	13	14	18	19	19	21	24	10	11	12	13	15	15	16	21
		10	16	20	21	23	25	25	28	38	13	14	16	19	21	21	23	27	11	12	14	15	17	17	20	23

‡ Box width (the dimension away from the body) (cm).
§ Vertical distance of lift (cm).
¶ Percentage of industrial population.
Italicized values exceed 8 h physiological criteria (see text).

Table A3-3: MAXIMUM ACCEPTABLE WEIGHT OF LOWER FOR MALES (kg)

Width‡	Distance§	Percent¶	Knuckle height to floor level — One lower every								Shoulder height to knuckle height — One lower every								Arm reach to shoulder height — One lower every							
			5	9 s	14	1	2 min	5	30	8 h	5	9 s	14	1	2 min	5	30	8 h	5	9 s	14	1	2 min	5	30	8 h
75	76	90	7	9	10	12	14	15	16	20	10	11	14	14	15	15	16	19	6	7	9	9	10	10	11	13
		75	10	13	14	18	20	22	22	29	13	16	18	18	21	21	21	26	9	10	12	12	14	14	14	18
		50	14	17	19	23	27	29	30	38	18	20	24	24	27	27	28	34	11	13	15	16	18	18	19	23
		25	17	21	24	29	33	36	37	47	21	25	29	29	34	34	34	42	14	16	19	20	23	23	23	28
		10	20	25	28	34	39	42	44	56	25	29	34	34	39	39	39	49	16	19	22	23	26	26	27	33
	51	90	8	10	11	13	15	16	17	21	11	12	14	15	17	17	18	22	7	8	9	10	12	12	12	15
		75	11	14	15	18	21	23	23	30	14	17	20	21	24	24	24	30	9	11	13	14	16	16	16	20
		50	14	18	20	24	28	30	31	40	19	21	25	27	31	31	31	38	12	14	15	18	21	21	21	26
		25	18	22	25	30	34	37	39	49	23	26	31	33	38	38	38	47	15	17	20	22	26	26	26	32
		10	21	26	29	36	41	44	46	58	27	31	36	38	44	44	44	55	17	20	24	26	30	30	30	37
	25	90	9	11	12	15	17	18	19	24	12	14	17	18	21	21	21	26	8	9	11	12	14	14	14	17
		75	13	16	17	21	24	25	26	34	17	20	23	24	28	28	28	35	11	13	15	16	19	19	19	24
		50	17	21	23	27	31	34	35	45	22	25	30	32	36	36	37	45	14	16	19	21	24	24	25	31
		25	21	26	29	34	39	42	44	56	27	31	37	39	44	44	45	56	17	20	24	26	30	30	30	38
		10	24	31	34	40	46	49	51	66	31	36	43	45	52	52	52	65	20	23	28	30	35	35	35	44
49	76	90	8	10	11	15	17	18	19	24	10	11	14	14	15	15	16	19	7	8	10	11	12	12	12	15
		75	12	15	16	21	24	26	26	34	13	16	18	18	21	21	21	26	10	11	14	15	17	17	17	21
		50	15	19	21	27	31	34	35	45	18	20	24	24	27	27	28	34	13	15	17	19	22	22	22	27
		25	19	24	26	34	39	42	44	56	21	25	29	29	34	34	34	42	16	18	21	23	27	27	27	33
		10	23	28	31	40	46	49	51	65	25	29	34	34	39	39	39	49	18	21	25	27	31	31	31	39
	51	90	9	11	12	15	17	19	19	25	11	12	14	15	17	17	18	22	8	9	10	12	14	14	14	17
		75	13	15	17	22	25	26	28	35	14	17	20	21	24	24	24	30	10	12	14	16	19	19	19	24
		50	16	20	22	29	33	35	37	47	19	21	25	27	31	31	31	38	14	16	18	21	24	24	25	31
		25	20	25	27	36	41	44	46	58	23	26	31	33	38	38	38	47	17	19	23	26	30	30	30	37
		10	23	29	32	42	48	51	54	68	27	31	36	38	44	44	44	55	19	22	26	30	35	35	35	44
	25	90	10	13	13	17	20	21	22	28	12	14	17	18	21	21	21	26	9	10	12	14	16	16	16	20
		75	14	18	19	24	28	30	31	40	17	20	23	24	28	28	28	35	12	14	17	19	22	22	22	28
		50	19	23	25	32	37	40	41	54	22	25	30	32	36	36	37	45	16	18	21	25	29	29	29	36
		25	23	29	31	40	46	49	51	65	27	31	37	39	44	44	45	56	20	23	27	31	35	35	36	44
		10	27	34	37	47	55	58	60	77	31	36	43	45	52	52	52	65	23	26	31	36	41	41	42	52
34	76	90	10	12	13	17	19	21	21	27	11	12	14	15	17	17	18	22	9	10	12	12	14	14	14	18
		75	14	17	19	24	27	29	30	39	14	17	20	21	24	24	24	30	12	13	16	17	19	19	19	24
		50	18	23	25	32	36	40	40	51	19	21	25	27	31	31	31	38	15	17	21	22	25	25	25	31
		25	23	29	31	39	45	48	50	64	23	26	31	33	38	38	38	47	19	21	25	27	31	31	31	38
		10	27	34	37	46	53	57	59	75	27	31	36	38	44	44	44	55	22	25	30	31	36	36	36	45
	51	90	10	13	14	17	20	21	22	29	11	13	15	17	20	20	20	24	9	10	12	14	16	16	16	20
		75	14	18	19	24	28	30	32	40	15	18	21	23	27	27	27	33	12	14	16	19	22	22	22	27
		50	19	24	26	33	37	40	42	53	20	23	27	30	35	35	35	43	16	19	21	24	28	28	28	35
		25	23	30	33	41	47	50	52	67	24	28	33	37	42	42	43	53	20	23	25	30	34	34	35	43
		10	27	35	38	48	55	59	62	78	28	33	39	43	49	49	50	62	23	27	30	35	40	40	40	50
	25	90	12	15	16	20	23	24	25	32	13	15	18	20	23	23	23	29	11	12	15	16	19	19	19	23
		75	17	21	23	28	32	34	36	46	18	21	25	27	31	31	32	39	15	17	20	22	26	26	26	32
		50	23	28	31	37	42	46	47	60	23	27	32	35	41	41	41	51	19	22	26	29	33	33	33	41
		25	28	35	38	46	53	57	59	75	29	33	39	43	50	50	50	63	23	27	32	35	41	41	41	51
		10	33	41	45	54	62	67	70	89	33	39	46	51	58	58	59	73	27	31	37	41	47	47	48	59

‡ Box width (the dimension away from the body) (cm).
§ Vertical distance of lower (cm).
¶ Percentage of industrial population.
Italicized values exceed 8 h physiological criteria (see text).

Table A3-4: MAXIMUM ACCEPTABLE WEIGHT OF LOWER FOR FEMALES (kg)

Width‡	Distance§	Percent¶	Knuckle height to floor level — One lower every								Shoulder height to knuckle height — One lower every								Arm reach to shoulder height — One lower every							
			5 s	9 s	14 s	1 min	2 min	5 min	30 min	8 h	5 s	9 s	14 s	1 min	2 min	5 min	30 min	8 h	5 s	9 s	14 s	1 min	2 min	5 min	30 min	8 h
75	76	90	5	6	7	7	8	8	9	12	6	6	7	8	9	10	10	13	5	5	5	6	7	7	7	9
		75	6	7	8	8	10	10	11	14	7	8	8	10	11	12	12	15	6	6	6	7	9	8	8	11
		50	7	9	10	11	12	12	13	17	8	9	9	11	13	15	15	18	6	8	8	8	10	10	10	13
		25	9	11	12	13	14	14	15	20	9	11	11	13	15	17	17	21	8	9	9	10	11	12	12	15
		10	10	13	13	14	16	16	17	23	11	12	13	15	17	19	19	24	9	10	10	11	12	14	14	17
	51	90	6	7	8	8	9	9	10	14	7	8	8	9	10	11	11	14	5	6	6	7	7	8	8	10
		75	7	8	9	10	11	11	13	17	8	9	9	11	12	13	13	17	6	7	7	9	9	10	10	12
		50	8	10	11	12	14	14	15	20	10	11	11	13	15	16	16	20	7	8	8	10	11	12	12	15
		25	10	12	13	14	16	16	18	24	11	13	13	15	17	19	19	23	8	9	9	11	12	13	13	17
		10	11	13	14	16	18	18	20	27	13	15	15	17	19	21	21	26	9	11	11	12	14	15	15	19
	25	90	6	8	8	9	10	10	11	14	8	8	8	10	11	11	12	15	6	6	6	7	8	8	9	11
		75	8	10	10	11	12	12	14	17	9	11	11	12	14	14	16	19	7	7	7	9	9	11	11	13
		50	9	11	12	13	15	15	16	21	11	13	13	15	17	17	18	22	7	8	9	10	11	12	12	16
		25	11	13	14	15	17	17	19	25	13	15	15	17	19	19	20	26	9	10	10	12	13	13	15	18
		10	12	15	16	17	19	19	21	28	15	17	17	19	21	21	23	29	10	12	12	13	15	15	16	21
49	76	90	5	6	7	8	8	9	10	13	8	6	7	8	9	10	10	13	5	5	5	6	7	7	8	10
		75	6	8	8	9	10	11	12	16	9	8	8	10	11	11	12	15	6	6	6	8	9	8	9	12
		50	8	9	10	11	12	13	14	19	11	9	10	12	13	13	14	18	6	8	8	9	11	9	11	14
		25	9	11	12	13	15	15	17	22	13	11	11	13	15	15	16	21	8	9	9	10	12	11	13	16
		10	11	13	13	15	17	18	19	25	15	12	13	15	17	17	19	24	9	10	10	12	13	13	15	19
	51	90	6	7	7	8	10	10	11	14	7	8	8	10	10	11	11	14	5	6	6	7	8	8	9	11
		75	7	8	9	10	12	12	13	17	8	9	9	11	13	13	14	17	6	7	7	9	10	10	11	13
		50	8	10	11	12	15	15	16	20	10	11	11	13	15	16	16	20	7	9	9	10	12	12	13	16
		25	10	12	13	15	16	16	18	23	11	13	13	15	17	19	19	23	8	10	10	12	13	15	15	18
		10	11	13	14	17	19	20	21	26	13	15	15	17	19	21	21	26	9	12	12	13	15	16	16	21
	25	90	6	8	8	9	10	11	12	15	8	8	8	10	11	11	12	15	6	6	7	8	9	9	9	12
		75	8	10	10	11	13	13	14	19	10	11	11	12	14	14	16	20	7	9	8	9	11	11	12	14
		50	9	11	12	14	16	16	17	23	11	13	13	15	16	16	18	23	8	9	10	11	13	13	14	17
		25	11	14	14	16	18	19	20	27	14	15	15	17	19	19	20	26	9	11	11	13	14	16	16	20
		10	13	15	16	18	20	21	23	30	16	17	17	19	21	21	23	30	11	12	12	14	16	18	18	23
34	76	90	6	8	8	9	10	10	12	15	8	8	8	10	11	11	12	15	7	6	7	8	9	9	9	13
		75	8	10	10	11	13	13	14	19	10	11	11	12	15	15	16	19	8	9	8	10	12	12	12	16
		50	10	11	13	13	16	16	18	23	11	13	13	15	16	18	20	23	9	11	11	13	14	14	16	19
		25	11	14	14	16	18	19	20	27	15	15	15	17	19	21	24	27	11	13	13	14	16	16	18	22
		10	13	16	16	18	21	22	23	30	16	17	17	19	23	24	27	30	13	15	15	16	18	18	20	23
	51	90	7	9	9	11	11	12	14	18	9	9	9	11	12	12	13	17	7	8	8	10	11	11	11	15
		75	9	11	11	13	13	15	17	22	11	13	13	14	15	15	16	21	8	10	10	12	13	13	15	18
		50	11	13	13	16	16	19	20	27	13	15	15	17	18	20	22	25	10	11	11	13	15	15	18	21
		25	12	14	14	19	19	21	24	31	15	15	15	18	21	23	26	29	11	13	13	14	16	18	19	24
		10	14	16	17	21	22	24	27	35	17	17	17	21	23	26	29	32	12	15	15	16	18	20	22	28
	25	90	8	10	11	11	13	13	14	19	9	9	9	11	12	12	13	17	8	8	8	9	11	11	12	15
		75	10	12	13	14	16	16	17	23	11	13	13	15	16	16	18	21	10	9	10	11	13	14	14	18
		50	12	14	15	17	19	20	21	28	14	15	15	17	18	20	23	25	11	11	11	14	15	17	17	21
		25	14	17	18	20	23	23	24	33	17	17	17	20	23	23	24	29	13	13	13	16	18	19	19	24
		10	15	19	20	22	26	26	28	37	17	17	17	21	26	26	28	32	15	15	15	18	20	22	22	28

‡ Box width (the dimension away from the body) (cm).
§ Vertical distance of lower (cm).
¶ Percentage of industrial population.
Italicized values exceed 8 h physiological criteria (see text).

Table A3-5: MAXIMUM ACCEPTABLE WEIGHT OF CARRY (kg)

Height‡	Percent§	2.1 m carry — One carry every							4.3 m carry — One carry every							8.5 m carry — One carry every						
		6 s	12 s	1 min	2 min	5 min	30 min	8 h	10 s	16 s	1 min	2 min	5 min	30 min	8 h	18 s	24 s	1 min	2 min	5 min	30 min	8 h
Males																						
111	90	10	14	17	17	19	21	25	9	11	15	15	17	19	22	10	11	13	13	15	17	20
	75	14	19	23	23	26	29	34	13	16	21	21	23	26	30	13	15	18	18	20	23	27
	50	19	25	30	30	33	38	44	17	20	27	27	30	34	39	17	19	23	24	26	29	35
	25	23	30	37	37	41	46	54	20	25	33	33	37	41	48	21	24	29	29	32	36	43
	10	27	35	43	43	48	54	63	24	29	38	39	43	48	57	24	28	34	34	38	42	50
79	90	13	17	21	21	23	26	31	11	14	18	19	21	23	27	13	15	17	18	20	22	26
	75	18	23	28	29	32	36	42	16	19	25	25	28	32	37	17	20	24	24	27	30	35
	50	23	30	37	37	41	46	54	20	25	32	33	36	41	48	22	26	31	31	35	39	46
	25	28	37	45	46	51	57	67	25	30	40	40	45	50	59	27	32	38	38	42	48	56
	10	33	43	53	53	59	66	78	29	35	47	47	52	59	69	32	38	44	45	50	56	65
Females																						
105	90	11	12	13	13	13	13	18	9	10	13	13	13	13	18	10	11	12	12	12	12	16
	75	13	14	15	15	16	16	21	11	12	15	15	16	16	21	12	13	14	14	14	14	19
	50	15	16	18	18	18	18	25	12	13	18	18	18	18	24	14	15	16	16	16	16	22
	25	17	18	20	20	21	21	28	14	15	20	20	21	21	28	15	17	18	18	19	19	25
	10	19	20	22	22	23	23	31	16	17	22	22	23	23	31	17	19	20	20	21	21	28
72	90	13	14	16	16	16	16	22	10	11	14	14	14	14	20	12	12	14	14	14	14	19
	75	15	17	18	18	19	19	25	11	13	16	16	16	17	23	14	15	16	16	17	17	23
	50	17	19	21	21	22	22	29	13	15	19	19	20	20	26	16	17	19	19	20	20	26
	25	20	22	24	24	25	25	33	15	17	22	22	22	22	30	18	19	21	22	22	22	30
	10	22	24	27	27	28	28	37	17	19	24	24	25	25	33	20	21	24	24	25	25	33

‡ Vertical distance from floor to hands (cm).
§ Percentage of industrial population.
Italicized values exceed 8 h physiological criteria (see text).

SELECTED BIBLIOGRAPHY

References to specific texts and other technical literature in Ergonomics have generally been excluded from the present manuscript for readability and because the material is of a generalized nature not extracted from any specific source. For those who wish to read further, however, the following books, in alphabetical order by author, are suggested. A short list of resource journals commonly referred to by ergonomic practitioners is also provided.

Books

1. Eastman Kodak Company, Human Factors Section: *Ergonomic Design for People at Work.* London, Singapore, Sydney, Toronto, Mexico City, Wadsworth Inc., 1983, and subsequent.
2. Fraser, T. Morris: *The Worker at Work.* London, New York, Philadelphia, Taylor and Francis, 1989.
3. Grandjean, Etienne: *Fitting the Task to the Man,* 4th ed. London, New York, Philadelphia, Taylor and Francis, 1988.
4. McCormick, Ernest J., Sanders, Mark S.: *Human Factors Engineering and Design,* 5th ed. New York, London, Toronto, etc., McGraw Hill Book Company, 1982.
5. Murrell, K.F.H.: *Ergonomics: Man in His Working Environment,* 6th ed. New York, John Wiley & Sons, Inc., 1979.
6. National Institute of Occupational Safety and Health: *Work Practices Guide for Manual Lifting,* Cincinnati, Oh., NIOSH, 1981.
7. Van Cott, Harold P. and Robert G. Kinkade: *Human Engineering Guide to Equipment Design,* revised ed. Washington, D.C., American Institutes for Research, U.S. Government Printing Office, 1972.

Journals

1. *Applied Ergonomics.* Butterworth and Company. Surrey, England.
2. *Ergonomics.* Taylor and Francis. London, England.
3. *Human Factors.* Human Factors Society, Inc. Santa Monica, USA.
4. *International Journal of Industrial Ergonomics.* Elsevier Science Publishers. Amsterdam, Oxford, New York and Tokyo.

INDEX